ORIGINAL
INNOCENCE

Other Works By Traktung Yeshe Dorje

Eye to Form is Only Love ~ *A Journal of 100 Days*
For 100 days, Traktung Yeshe Dorje kept a journal of short
reflections. Some mornings, the heartbreaking poetry of
devotion, or essays in celebration of dawn, light, trees; on
others, razor-like distinctions about the nature of the mind,
challenges to conventional views of seeing, or seething commentary on the shallowness of contemporary culture. Taken
together, but in small considered bites, the entries provide a
rare meal to any sincere practitioner who recognizes direct
and authentic spiritual discourse.
Hohm Press, 2012, ISBN: 978-1-935387-29-9, $16.95

In the Woods of Nowhere by Just A Tourist (lyrics by
Traktung Yeshe Dorje), *Honey Rain: Meditation Songs of
Tibetan Masters*, and many other CDs produced by Dzam
Studios under the guidance of Traktung Yeshe Dorje are now
available for free download at www.dzamstudio.com

ORIGINAL
INNOCENCE

TRAKTUNG YESHE DORJE

Hohm Press
Chino Valley, Arizona

Cover/Interior Design: Zac Parker, zdpdigitalmedia@gmail.com

Library of Congress Cataloging-in-Publication Data

Traktung Yeshe Dorje, author.
Original innocence / Traktung Yeshe Dorje.
    pages cm
Includes bibliographical references.
ISBN 978-1-935387-55-8 (trade pbk. : alk. paper)
1. Spiritual life--Tantric Buddhism. I. Title.
BQ8938.T73 2014
294.3'444--dc23
                              2013049118

Hohm Press
P.O. Box 4410
Chino Valley, AZ 86323
800-381-2700
www.hohmpress.com

This book was printed in the U.S.A. on recycled, acid-free paper using soy ink.

Permission credits for poetry cited in this book are found on page 195.

Dedicated to my beloved Khandro,
source of joy and wisdom.

CONTENTS

PROLOGUE

Digestivo: Noun (plural digestive /-vi/): a drink, especially an alcoholic one, drunk before or after a meal in order to aid the digestion.

A scholar comes to a sage, knocks on his door, enters and begins conversation. He speaks and speaks of what he has learned, information he has gathered, opinions, ideas, descriptions. The sage makes some food and feeds the scholar. He feeds him more and more and the scholar, out of politeness, eats. Finally the scholar blurts out, "If I eat another bite I will vomit. How am I supposed to digest this absurd meal?" The sage laughs gently and replies, "Yes, exactly. This is exactly what I was thinking about your accumulated knowledge. Come and I will show you the secret of digestion."
 – Dakini Tsog, 1st day of the Sturgeon Moon, 2013

Illusion's beer, its miracle blessing,
runs down the throat of preparation,
intoxicating and delighting,
the mind of vast accomplishment.
Those with the nerve and dauntless courage,
that comes with quaffing this strong beverage,
cannot be conquered by illusory phantoms,
cannot be hindered by illusion's Game.
They are the victors, chariot drivers,
of Vajrayana's splendid vehicle.
 – Jamgon Kongtrul Lodro Thaye

PART I
ORIGINAL INNOCENCE

And I shall have some peace there, for peace comes dropping slow,
Dropping from the veils of the morning to where the cricket sings;
There midnight's all a glimmer, and noon a purple glow,
And evening full of the linnet's wings.
                    – "The Lake Isle of Innisfree," William Butler Yeats

Well then … A sage is mystery that is untouched by being or non-being, A sage is neither human, nor god, nor demon. They are the fragrance of a flower.

Buddha was asked, "Are you human?" – he replied, "No." He was also not a god, a demon, or other "thing." Buddha was not claiming status horn of separation between this and that; Buddha was not that fretful kind who garnered surety from falsehood. His truth was beyond both surety and falsehood. He was not speaking of only or alone (only Me, I alone). Buddha spoke of What Is – Always already –; though perhaps unseen, unnoticed. And, in that unnoticing, much is arising – worlds, realms, persons, hopes, fears and the anxiety of being.

Perceiving across expanse … (no "one" perceiving, no "thing" perceived and yet mystery beyond word or concept … perceiving across expanse). That is all. Light arising without cause from no "place" to no "where." This "I" this "you" this "we" made from stuff more gossamer than dreams.

Buddha, the Nazarene, Padmasambhava, Radha, Lee, Ikkyū, Hildegard, Arnaud, Meister Eckhart, Yeshe Tsogyel, Basho, this body … unnoticed things, unmade being, welcomed mystery. Wisdom's sunlight suffuses, pervades, identity falls away like mist embraced by the rays of dawn's bright warmth.

Perceiving plants a thousand times a thousand flower seeds in the expanse of possibility. Some seeds sprout, grow, blossom – and in the blossoming of unknowing, unmaking, unnoticing, the fragrance is shared. It is a welcoming. It is an invitation.

How astonishing! This phenomena is superb!
It is the secret of all the fully enlightened Buddhas!
Everything is born from the unborn;
at the moment of birth nothing is born.

– *Guyagharba Tantra*

The current notion that one cannot escape one's destiny is
applicable only to weak minded and senseless wastrels.

– *Tripura Rahasya*, 7.62.

Appearance Is the Kingdom of Virtue

Appearance is exactly where non-duality is found.
Appearance arisen from the union of emptiness and clarity;
this is the freedom place.

If you look for the ground of all phenomena you will not
find anything at all. Precisely this looking and not finding
is the ground of all phenomena. Train the mind to be like
space. Then forget space.

Mind's activity is a phenomena. Mind's deep, a groundlessness. Phenomena and mind's activity share in common the
baseless groundlessness. Again and again rest mind's hurried
activity in the expanse of its ownmost non-doing.

Mind's deep, a groundlessness, is Original Innocence.
Phenomena, also groundless, are Bright Virtue. If you
understand these two you will swiftly master the Buddha's
twofold path of Shamatha and Vipassana.

Original Innocence. The Deep

Original Innocence is the very essence of your mind. Feel it for a moment. Not suffering, not frustration, hope or fear but Original Innocence. Not original sin but Original Innocence. When great mystics and sages come to discover the deepest essence of reality this is what they discover. Their words may vary, the flowering of this realization may find different expression but the essence remains the same because it is truth.

The mind's day-to-day conceptual functioning is merely the tip of an iceberg. The sum total of your day to-day identity, even the whole appearing called the human realm, is the very tip of an iceberg. Beneath this tiny tip is a vast and deep expanse of spiritual mystery. The tip, the day-to-day conundrum, is like the foam on the edge of a rising wave; but your essence is like the ocean's depth. This truth, and the methods to realize it – to make it real in the continuum of your body, feeling, mind, qualities and actions – is the intent of every Buddha's, every mystic's, communication. It is the sole import of the sage's speech and activity.

Mind's essence, timelessly – right now, always, is an expanse of unchanging Original Innocence. Somewhere, deep within, all beings intuit this, and this intuition is precisely what draws the body, mind and heart toward spiritual seeking. The wave is never separate from the ocean. If the wave forgot its union with the ocean and only felt itself to be a separate movement of water, what anxiety it would suffer! It would feel itself to be so temporary, so momentary and at the whim of rise and fall, birth and death. It would desperately search for meaning within the minute span of its existence, not knowing that its meaning is an expression of the deep and not found in and of its shortness. Original Innocence is a meaning-saturated field opening into the ceaseless possibilities of expression through the energies of appearing, but if the deep connection to Original Innocence is lost an anxious search begins. The search in its immaturity is for partial temporary meanings within the momentary dimension of appearing. As maturity grows it becomes a search for direct knowing of the meaning-saturated ownmostness of mind itself. The search is to discover what has always already been the case.

Although the sky appears grey when covered over with clouds it is still blue above the clouds. The clouds are simply adventitious stains, temporary. If you fly up in a plane you can see that there is always already blueness, a stainless sky ultimately unharmed by temporary clouds. The moon waxes and wanes from the point of view of earth, but when seen from the perspective of space it is always full. It is only "point of view" that creates partiality. In the same way, the reality of our deepest nature is always divine. It is not divine in seed form, like a tree waiting to grow from a seed, but fully developed, right now.

My father had a friend who became mentally deranged during WWII. He thought he was Napoleon. Little by little he was brought back to health, but the truth, the actual TRUTH, of who he was remained exactly the same throughout the continuum from sickness to health. The TRUTH of who he was adhered as the ground of his psychological recovery. The path was to remove the obstacles to seeing this truth. The result was to inhabit the truth.

This is exactly the way of the Tantric path. The ground of the path is your Original Innocence. The work of the path is to remove the obstacles to seeing what is always already true. The result of the path is to inhabit this truth. The ground and the result are one and the same. For this reason the Tantric path is referred to as "the resultant path." If the path were to give you something you had not had before, then it could be lost. If it were to take you back to some garden you had been expelled from you could again be thrown out. At the same time without the path one remains in ignorance of reality, for the path is nothing other than reality's communication to us in the endarkened realm of confusion's homeland.

You should wholly sink away from your you-ness and
dissolve into His His-ness, and your "yours" and His "His"
should become so completely one "Mine" that with Him
you understand His unbecome Is-ness and His nameless
Nothing-ness.

– Meister Eckhart

∽

Thus it is. Just as the intrinsic nature of fire is to be hot so the
intrinsic nature of phenomena is primordially blessed as the
mandala of the awakened ones.

– Longchenpa

∽

Since the unknowing of what is beyond being is something
above and beyond speech, mind, or being itself, one should
ascribe to it an understanding beyond being.

– Pseudo-Dionysius

∽

From the time I achieved fully enlightened Buddhahood
until passing into Nirvana I never taught the Dharma.
Nevertheless, this is the inconceivable blessing secret of the
Buddha's speech that even untaught it is heard in accord
with the need of each being.

– from the sutra known as
The Inconceivable Amassing of Rare and Supreme

∽

my chest broke open
and the Love bird flew to the moon.
your cloak became the sky   midnight blue
                flecks of gold
                the bright of stars.
everywhere i look   spiral of little shells
the turning of the heart   in Love.

the moon came to live in my chest   the mantle
                of its light
formed a cradle for my mind
and Silence, like a crown,
        o
        r
        n
        a
        m
        e
        n
        t
        e
        d   the vertigo of this love.

my chest broke open
and the love bird flew to the moon.

Bright Virtue. The Expanse

Original Innocence is untouched and untouchable. It is perfect mystery. You can not even know it for it can not be an object of knowledge grasped by a subjective knower. Long before it is realized fully both knower and known dissolve in perfect unutterable mystery. This is why in our Nyingma lineage there is, right from the start, the distinction between wisdom and experience.

Original Innocence is unspeakable mystery. It is untouched by any concept. It is beyond the reach of even those most fundamental axioms of concept "Is" and "Is not." It is beyond being and non-being, it is beyond the "I Am." It is always unknowable, but it is realizable, and perfectly devoid of, free from, concepts. It is without attribute, color, substance, being, non-being, both being and non-being, neither being or non-being, characteristic or quality .... What can be seen and the seer are not it, what can be known and the knower are not it – and yet it is Beingness's deepest TRUTH.

This unutterable mystery is, for no reason at all, uncaused yet spontaneously pervaded by luminous clarity replete with potential qualities. Like clear light that contains the rainbow spectrum within it. The perfect mystery that is Original Innocence is also uncharacterized by any dimensionality, so how can its expanse be pervaded by luminosity when its expanse is dimensionless? The essence is unspeakable mystery and the nature of that mystery is radiant luminosity. The very radiance of its nature creates the expanse in-as-of its radiance. The essence is perfect purity and innocence and the nature is a clear light radiance. Why is it like this? For absolutely no reason. This is simply how it is. When yogis look directly into the essence and nature of reality this is what is discovered.

What must be understood is that the heart of wisdom is Original Innocence and Bright Virtue – this authentic reality of Buddha Nature has also, from the start, been the very basis of mind's natural state … and that basis is no basis at all but pure, divine, substanceless, ineffable perfection of wisdom mystery. This basis of mind's deepest reality is a mystery beyond all notions and all concepts such as birth, death, being, non-being, color, attribute, shape and size. It is an expanse of sublime spiritual mystery. When we come to recognize our own mind's deepest reality we will have come to know the Original Innocence and Bright Virtue of the divine. Even more profound and amazing is that when this deep reality of mind is known the truth of all appearances is also known – the manner in which all appearances are held in-as-of this very expanse. Everywhere and every when, ev ery appearance, always only forever is nothing other than the ornament of primordial purity and luminous spontaneity.

The luminous expanse we call Bright Virtue. It is un-caused, it is luminous and radiant and it is replete with po-tential qualities that are known and made actual in the mind and life of the meditator. The mystery in Tantra, is called "the essence of awareness," and Bright Virtue is often called "the nature of awareness." The union of these two gives birth, as unions often do, to a child, which is the unceasing magi-cal dimension of appearing that is often called the "energy of awareness."

This triune synergy is, of course, undivided wholeness. The yogin, when meditating on the essence, rests in perfect non-conceptual non-elaboration. Then they realize the emp-tiness and nothingness (no-thing-ness) aspects of reality. When they abide in meditation upon the luminous aspect they see, perfectly and always, the divinity of appearing and appearances. Then they know the godliness of everything and every thing. The pin-prick of appearance that is the sage's body abides in the paradoxical union of these two. Emptiness and godliness are like a swing on which the magical child of illusion plays as love.

The essence, nature and energy of awareness is also known in Tantra as the three *kayas* or bodies of a Buddha. They are referred to as Dharmakaya, Sambhogakaya, and Nirmanakaya respectively. Dharmakaya is the perfect mystery of awareness that is unspeakable. Sambhogakaya's name translates as *Sam* (great), *Bhoga* (Pleasure/bliss) and *Kaya* (body). So Sambhogakaya is the body or dimension of visionary beauty and wonder. Nirmanakaya is, quite simply, Love. Not as a static state, but love in action as appearance and the action of appearing. It is how wisdom bliss becomes an array of playful forms, like waves rising and falling. Dharmakaya is the ocean. Sambhogakaya is the ocean's tremendous tidal force, and Nirmanakaya is the wave of appearance rising and falling.

The essence, originally pure wisdom,
is free from ignorance and all thoughts.
The nature, spontaneously present wisdom,
is empty clarity suffused with luminosity.
The energy, a compassion display of wisdom,
is unceasing magical appearance.

– Gyü Long Sal

∽

The Buddha's kayas, wisdoms, qualities as well as sentient
beings' karmas, habit patterns and all that – every possible
appearance, worlds, beings, from the very start these have all
been great awareness.

– *Künje Gyalpo Tantra*

∽

Those who see me as form and hear my voice enter the path
wrongly. All Buddhas should be seen as the nature of all
phenomena and all guides as the Dharmakaya. The nature of
Truth is not a knowable *thing*. So it is incomprehensible.

– *The Vajra Cutter Tantra*

∽

All phenomena are unborn and spontaneously perfect.
When primordial freedom is realized, all motivation and
activity is spontaneously accomplished … and the perfect
nature appears without being created.

– *The Greatness of Space Tantra*

∽

The single taste of luminous clarity

2 AM, vomiting. walking from bathroom to bed i glance
down and, inside my shirt, only stars and moonlight.
5 AM, laying on the bathroom floor wondering if viruses are
living beings, a single thought of love and this old karmic
body is filled with warmth.
7 AM, skin aches to the bone, remembering Milarepa's poem,
"feels good, feels even better, feels so good even feeling bad
feels good."
dharma's promise never falls short.

Awareness writes jazz compositions on the paper of *dharma-
ta* with the ink of luminosity.

One of the truly great joys of having abandoned identity is
the spontaneous play-full-ness of awareness across sense
fields. When hope and fear fall away, as they depend on
identity for survival, then appearance, the perceiving of it
and the falling away of it are all known as only the three
bodies of a Buddha.

and the name is Love

I had just written the lines: *"The day I met you I realized all love poems are just different ways to spell your name."*

And the man beside me, glancing at them, said "Buddhists don't write love poems." I replied, "If that were the case then there would be no appearance."

What do you think appearance is if not a love poem written on the paper of VastExpanse with the ink of WisdomBliss by the hand of no-thing-ness.

Emptiness doesn't mean we are unfeeling – just unfooled.

Love is not desire,
not grasping,
not attachment,

it is sunlight played from heart to eye ...... and ......

without implication of birth ...... and yet "replete with qualities."

The moment I met you I knew language's secret purpose: to discover a million ways to write your name.

The Magical Child. The Energy

In short, all appearances are not other than the spiritual potency of mind's great mystery and mind itself has no basis. This is because appearance is the union of the empty and luminous essence and the nature of the mind. This emptiness has no basis – it is perfect mystery. The luminous aspect is spontaneous, without cause, also having no basis. What a lark! What a joy that when truth is sought with no ulterior motive other than seeking truth, this perfect mystery is what has been discovered by men and women from myriad traditions in all times and cultures.

When I was in my late teens and embarking on my spiritual journey in search of truth, my mother, who was very intelligent and well read in psychology and philosophy, asked me, "What if the 'truth' is not something you can live with, something terrible?" I replied, "I don't really care because I must know." That is the attitude one must maintain on the journey so as not to superimpose a particular result. And what a joy that of all possible outcomes, what is discovered in the depths of being human is a tri-fold wholeness of divinity that is realizable and livable. It is the function of the path to awaken you to this subtle wisdom understanding, but the wisdom itself has always been true from the beginning. Wisdom is to discover and then inhere in-and-as this truth.

The spiritual longing of every human being is to realize, make real in the continuum of life, body, speech, mind, this reality. To embody and enworld the beauty of Buddha Nature's expanse and luminous clarity is the "meaning urge" of our lives. The essence of spiritual reality, which is also the essence of mind, is an expanse of unutterable mystery – it is perfect purity. The nature of this purity is luminosity whose radiance is a perfect clarity. Original Innocence and Bright

Virtue are patiently waiting for us to discover and live them to the point of being translated into them – into what you have always been but missed due to some temporary stains of vision and understanding.

When prince Siddhartha became Shakyamuni Buddha, his first words following enlightenment were, "How wondrous, how marvelous, all beings have been Buddha since the beginning." All whose minds have awakened to the marvelous illuminating nature and essence of mind's reality have experienced this same shock of wonder! They see inseparable union of Original Innocence and Bright Virtue, shining and appearing as galaxies, worlds, and beings arising from timelessness itself.

Everyone sees in accord with his own eyes. Therefore Buddhas see only Buddha. Nothing other than Buddha Nature is seen by Buddhas. There is no original sin, only some seeming individual beings mistaking their true nature for something dimmer and less free. Buddhas do not see any actually existent suffering. They see no death and no birth, only the play of wisdom bliss, only Original Innocence. In Buddhism there is no expulsion from the Garden of Eden. There is only distorted vision that is unable to see the way things are in Truth. The blessings of Buddhas and the path of Dharma are the methods that lead to clear seeing. Buddhas, in their uncompromising pure vision, invite us to share in their state.

We are not being asked to believe unquestioned dogma or to debate interesting philosophy. Here the invitation is to the methods that make the body, the mind and feeling into subtle tools for spiritual knowing. The path is not easy, it requires intelligence, courage, hard work and interdependence … but if one examines one's life, it can easily be seen that suffering is also not easy. When we truly long for an end of suffering, we have entered the path.

The singleness of spiritual reality is a perfect mystery that is deep like the ocean and vast like the sky. Its openness, which is an utter mystery beyond all language, is felt and known in body and mind as Original Innocence and the perfect freedom of expressiveness that is Bright Virtue. It is the essence of everything and everyone – of YOU. Original Innocence is not somewhere else but right here, and appearance itself is the divulgence of Bright Virtue. It is not some place else waiting to be found because then it could be lost. It is not something one needs to create – then it could, and eventually would, fall apart. It is the discovery of the nature of things as they are when seen with clarity that is free from delusion. And then life becomes the act of forging body, mind and expression into the further divulgence of this wonder. Knowing this Original Innocence, one instantly also comes to know the radiant spontaneous brightness that is the basis of all appearances as well. This discovery does not make one special in any way. It does not give one a feeling of status, for it perceives the equality of all appearing as simply Buddha. In reality, it makes one ordinary for the first time because it releases the clenched fist of ego's effort to be special. When Original Innocence and Bright Virtue are realized in body, life and action become the emblem of wisdom and love.

When the ground consciousness dissolves into Dharmakaya
then the aggregates that were born as body and mind break
open like a person stepping on an egg.

– Milarepa, in a song to Rechungpa

∞

And if ever you come to this cloud, and make a home there
and take up the work of love as I urge you, there is something else you must do as this cloud is above you, and between you and your God, you must put a cloud of forgetting
beneath you, between you and all the creatures that have
ever been made. The cloud of unknowing will perhaps leave
you with a feeling that you are far from God. But I assure
you, if it is authentic, only the absence of a cloud of forgetting between you and all creatures keeps you from God.

– from *The Cloud of Unkowing*

∞

The ground, the root, of all samsara and nirvana is the single
great primordial indestructible bindu. Since it is a ceaseless
beginning it is known as primordial. Since it is indivisible it
is known as indestructible.

– Third Karmapa

∞

Love abounds in all things,
excels from the depths to beyond the stars,
is lovingly disposed to all things.
She has given the king on high
the kiss of peace.

– Hildegard of Bingen, *"Caritas abundat"*

Tonight we dance in this temple of ruin. Footsteps circling like lovesick birds – the hidden companions, the seducers of twilight.

Tonight we dance in the priory of new dawn. Our bodies prised open by longing's revelation: Like magnolia blossoms on a hot summer's eve.

For there is no hiding from heartbreak. No way to outrun the messengers of sorrow. And the mind, just a tourist, in this *saha* realm.* But it lives in the deep of your vast skyheartmind.

Tonight we dance in this temple of ruin. Tonight I dance in the reveries of Love. Sorrows outshined in the wanting of my love. And I want the blood red of your delicate kisses. And I want the syllables that fall from your lips. And I want the thirst of a man in the desert. And I want the nakedness of your unflinching kindness

Tonight we dance in the temple of ruin. Laughter mixed with the fragments of my longing.

*Saha realm, the realm of human confusions known as "Endurance."

Spiritual practice is not a seeking for something new but, rather, the untangling of the perceptual mechanism of our delusion so that inherent reality can be seen "as it is." Without such practice, accomplished in the meat and bone of life, no amount of chatter, FB quotes, or proclamations about non-duality, love, buddha nature or awareness brings any freedom from delusion at all – all of that is simply the defense mechanism of delusion.

Relationships with people you never meet are pretty much always the marketplace of narcissistic fantasy. The perusing of, and commenting on, the spiritual blatherings of the internet is the same. It does not constitute a path nor the relationships therein a sangha.

If you are unable to find the truth right where you are, where else do you expect to find it?

– Zen Master Dogen

The Fun House World of Confusions

When mind's conceptual functioning and identity becomes unaware of its continuity with the deep mystery of its own Original Innocence and Bright Virtue, then it becomes a tangled confusion. The body and human world, as lived in-as-of this loss, is the embodiment and enworldment of confusions.

The fracturing of direct Gnostic knowingness into conceptual frameworks binds the tremendous energy of Original Innocence and Bright Virtue. This binding is an endarkening described by varying fixations of attention in narrow patterning. Identification with this attenuation and narrowing creates the realm and world of living. A sense of dis-ease, of being trapped, moves human behavior in search of a solution to the problem of "being." This confused urge, this search, displays of every human being. Mind's conceptual activity and the world shape one another like a river and its banks.

Thought, embodiment, enworldment shape and are shaped by one another. They are more than just related, they are expressions of one another. For this reason confusion, unenlightenment does not merely abide as a concept but as the structuring of that concept as life. This structuring process binds the energy of wisdom bliss. The recovery of that energy will require work at all levels of existence. Spiritual life is not an intellectual affair alone. Enlightenment is of the wholeness. Original Innocence and Bright Virtue are realized as much in the feet, hands, actions as in the mind's structure.

Again this Incarnation:
"*son droit non du nient en que elle demoure*" –
"Now this soul has her right name from the nothingness in
    which she rests."
                          – Marguerite Porete, *Mirror of Simple Souls**

1. She wrote me: "I am nobody, daughter of no one,
I am, and I am not, three pines,
green black against the dusk sky."

Simplicity confounds.

2. Thingness afflicts, it is the spirit's great sadness.
mind-heart longs … to unbecome, together in love.
I am and I am not,

even that thing called body.

3. She wrote me: "a sorrow spreads. its wound,
like the blood of first sex, an annihilation – a deification.
It places me in nothingness. uncreated, all things

again conform wholly to divinity.

4. The unremembering of names becomes
an estuary of meanings. if you were to take
the sum of all my words they would whisper
Beatrice's claim: "the heart melts."**

                    [continued with stanza break]

She wrote: "I am nobody, daughter of no one, "the
    unbecoming of things and
simplicity, even in that thing called body, world, loving.
I am the unknown one and the unknowing of all ones.
    For uncreated
I dwell and in dwelling all things are become again in
    brightness.

I read her words and mind like light shattered across
    expanse ....

.... this heart so bright and full becomes the round of
    stars and lives. Not "I"
or "you" but brightness only. Feet appear in worlds of beauty
    where unmaking
has again allowed the fullness that is loving. Hands touch,
    eyes see, lips sing
syllables of mystery, and heart forever stands within without
    unutterableness.

In this way the virus of unbecoming and resurrection is
    spread. In word, look, song, painting, story, chant,
    sculpture, wind's breeze. ***

* Marguerite Porete, French Beguine mystic, died in 1310.
** Beatrice of Nazareth, Flemish mystic 1200-1268, author of the *Seven Ways of Holy Love.*
*** Do Khyentse Yeshe Dorje wrote: "My incarnations will be thousands. As gurus, lay people, monks, bakers, even the breeze through trees, works of art, the words of unknown women."

Essence, Nature, Energy. The Indivisibility

The essence of awareness is spaciousness devoid of any attribute or quality. Awareness is indescribable, inconceivable because no concept or set of concepts can encapsulate it. The spacious vast is, however, not a mere nothingness. It is pregnant no-thingness brimming with infinite potentiality. It is spontaneously luminous. It is luminous radiance, the resonance of potentiality that shimmers and suffuses space the way wetness pervades water. This resonance of potentiality is the intentionless source of every quality of the divine. Awareness, wisdom, compassion, beauty, playfulness, love and creativity are all the radiance of Original Innocence and comprise Bright Virtue. Its potentiality becomes an actuality in the body, mind and feelings as one progresses on the path.

The Tantric path is practical spiritual alchemy. The lead of deluded qualities is transformed into the gold of unborn wisdom awareness – awareness of Original Innocence and Bright Virtue. Deluded concepts have no existence in and of themselves. They have no reality. All appearance, all appearing, flows from-of-as-in the wholeness of Original Innocence and Bright Virtue. So what is delusion? It is comprised of the infinite qualities of the luminous nature seen through the distorting fun-house mirror of confusion and delusion. It is wrong knowing. It is like an anorexic who sees herself as fat. She really, literally, sees her emaciated body as large and grotesque. So delusion is like an anorexic but in reverse. Deluded confusion sees Nirmanakaya, which is only the magical manifestation of love, as all kinds of unhappiness and happiness mixed together. Fortunately, for beings, it is much easier to alchemically change gold, which is only confusedly seen as lead, back into gold than it would be if it were actually lead. And yet, it is still very difficult.

The endless, ceaseless radiance of Original Innocence's own nature, this Bright Virtue, surges forth within the expanse of purity. It surges forth as the context of every content. This expanse of purity is the womb space of all Buddhas, of every now and every when of everything. This is the truth you are invited to realize via the methods of the path, utilizing the beauty and power of the methods, and through the transmission force and blessings of lineage and guru. You are invited to see things as they are in truth, without distortion. As It Is. That is the whole of it. When we see things, others, ourselves and the world As It Is, something remarkable is seen, known and lived.

All of these … Lineage, guru, methods and path arise as Buddha externally. Spiritual longing for realization is Buddha arising internally. The outer does not lead to the inner or vice versa. Both internal and external are brought together through the wholeness of the path, and the moment they meet they form a synergy that destroys even the notion of internal or external. The expanse of purity and the expanse of luminous clarity are like fire and its light or like sugar and its sweetness – a synergistic singularity of emptiness and clarity, a non-duality from whom the child of illusion is born. All of this, this seeming union, the seeming birth, is appearance that never ruptures the subtlety of authentic non-duality. When known, loved in truth, it is, as my friend Lee Lozowick called it, "Enlightened Duality."

In all appearance the child of illusion, which is a magical display of unimpeded and unceasing wonderment, arises from, in and as the indivisibility of Original Innocence and

Bright Virtue. Virtue is the kingdom of all appearance, its brightness within the space of vast openness. Appearance is exactly where we find non-duality – it is the only place. Appearance is the freedom place. If you are confused about appearance, or rejecting of appearance, or see anything other than purity and wonderment suffusing the expanse, then wisdom is as of yet immature.

When prince Siddhartha opened his eyes, the bright morning star of wisdom shone across the horizon of spiritual awakening. His mind, a construction of confused concepts, dissolved in luminous spaciousness. Mind's own-most true essence and nature were seen. A Buddha was born. Buddha's first words, his proclamation, his lion's roar, which was identical to that of all Buddhas at the moment of awakening, was, "How wondrous, how marvelous that all being have been, from the beginning, Buddha." In seeing this great truth, the interface of awareness' essence, nature and energy with mind, expressiveness and body, Buddha became perfect. This interface is the meaning of the term "Buddha" or the Tibetan word *Sangye*. The first syllable (*San*) means removal of all obstacles to seeing, and the second part (*gye*) means the expansion of all qualities.

In the nature of awareness qualities are potential and it is in awakening within Buddha that the potentialities become actualized. When this happens, teachings emerge as the natural, uncontrived, intentionless vector of compassion. When a rain cloud is full it does not need a contrived intention to shower down its blessing rainfall on the earth. When mind, expressiveness and body become the three *kayas* of the Buddha, compassion appears like a gentle spring rain. One of the original meanings of the word guru was "Pregnant Raincloud."

In seeing that all beings are Buddha and seeing that suffering beings experience suffering unnecessarily, teachings arise as the natural spontaneous responsiveness of compassion. Perfect Wisdom reveals itself as the teachings and methods of our path.

The Buddha does not exist and neither does the dharma; sentient beings never existed either. Whoever knows this will realize the nature of phenomena like space and swiftly become the best amongst beings.

– Sourceless Nature of All Phenomena Tantra

Leave your body as a corpse. Leave it without any owner. Leave your mind as space. Without even a single reference point.

– Machig Labdron

Who would then deny that when I am sipping tea in my tearoom I am swallowing the whole universe with it and that this very moment of my lifting the bowl to my lips is eternity itself transcending time and space?

– D.T. Suzuki

For however much grasping there is to characteristics, that is how long there will be worldly characteristics. Whenever things are known to be without characteristics, that is when worldliness will be transcended and everything will be known as the pure land of Kuntuzangpo. Then passions and world become indivisible.

– The Magnificent Lightning Tantra

INTERLUDE
PALATE CLEANSER

The Tao that can be spoken is not the eternal Tao.
The name that can be named is not the eternal name.
The nameless is the origin of Heaven and Earth.

– Tao Te Ching

It must be remembered that we are talking about a mystery beyond all words, time, space, place, locations, self, others, and objects. Although words might be subtly able to point in the direction of this truth, no word or concept can actually describe it. This is the truth of all utterances of realizers from any and all traditions. Words can describe what unenlightenment is or how the path is practiced; or, if they speak of Truth and Reality, they can be mythopoetic utterances. They are the poetry of happiness. The outrageous happiness of the realizer makes use of language and stretches it like saltwater taffy in an attempt to twist it into the form and meanings of the most subtle of the subtlemost.

It is important to remember that the words are a method and are not truth in and of themselves. They point, solicit, cajole, incite, provoke, seduce, finagle and draw forth innate wisdom but being able to parrot them is not the point. Parroting actually creates greater obstacles because we believe that our words are truth and then we have less interest in discovering and living this truth. For a person with genuine longing, secondhand truth will never suffice.

The poetry that arises from a being who is swooned in reality can take the form of words, actions, song, music, dance, silence, sitting doing nothing, working in the garden ... its forms are endless. When the sage's mind goes where no mind goes (conceptuality dissolves like mist in the sun leaving behind only identityless mind as radiance in body) then body is compelled to express reality and truth, godliness and divinity in everything it does. This expression always falls short of perfect for the "perfect expression" is, of course, the sum total of all appearing, past, present and future.

Communication is always, in one sense, an interruption in the perfect communion of stillness and silence. But, at the same time, words, dance, work, song, whatever arises spontaneously is the perfect symbolic presentation of luminously joyful wisdom expanse. Perhaps each poetic utterance is in fact the summation of all appearing, past, present and future. Wisdom speech is mysterious, for it issues forth from Dharmakaya's perfect mystery. It is luminous, for it is the nature of awareness' symbolic ebullience. It is powerful, it is potent *siddhi*, for it is compassion manifest.

So, words arise from great silence and stretch the very fabric of language. They twist and turn and almost tear language to divulge wonderment. All dharma is the mythopoetics of wisdom, a song of joy shimmering in an empty space of timeless time. Timeless time, that womb space of all time where Bright Virtue surges like the tidal forces in the ocean of Original Innocence.

This World Is

This world is how love clothes itself. Mystery is love
    undressed.
Silence reveals, song adorns.

Lovers understand the strategies of love's play-full-ness. They
    enumerate them:
    1. February's taciturn secrets, its clandestine stirrings.
    2. The mechanics enjoyment of what's under the hood.
    3. Nighttime's seduction of twilight ......
    4. ...... too many to list.
    5.

Love brings the understanding of nuance. How there is mystery and expanse The emptiness at the center of the bead.
How the necklace adorns but it is the emptiness that makes
this possible.
Experience is the clothing of expanse, the mystery that wears
it. Love, clothed in world, undresses for expanse in the twilight of doing, in the bedroom of unmaking.
The Lover
moves beyond
    behind
    within ......
Like a bead, we are empty at the center, an expanse, a place
for sunlight. Like the flower we are drunk on sunlight.
This emptiness. This love.
Before, and without, "I" or "you," this is how we live.

A Walk While Writing

Walking through the field's frost covered grasses 7 PM, mind was silent, eyes drank in the delicate crystalline structures and the dance of twilight over brown and white. I speak to the grasses, "Tell me of your love affair with sunlight." And they answer. "Look to the hollowness of our stem – how we bend in the wind, to the fearlessness of our dying each fall and the divinity of our resurrection in spring."

Hand reaches out, fingers touch frost and stem, cold invites, sunlight invokes. Body moves with ease through thickets of brambles, small trees and tall grass. The brain's insistence on concept was gone and yet the dialogue with nature continued in-of-as silence. The senses, movement, dimensionality all tremendously alive and yet devoid of the reflexivity called "sense of self."

When mind, discovering how to remain silent, stretches across appearance – benediction suffuses perception with tender-hearted delicacy. This discovery brings with it that fullness sought after in all seeking whether it is called worldly or religious. Seeking, with its imagined destinations, projections, hopes and fears can never know this delicacy of living wonder and yet, without disciplining the mechanisms of attention and concept, there also will be no discovery, for conceptuality's habit will shape mind and feeling.

There is brutality in the insistence of conceptuality's habits, its unrelenting pace and diminishment of joy, and this brutality is felt in the structures of modern life. There is also a great potential sensitivity in the brain's mechanism, a possible subtlety and the workings of organic and sacred intelligence. The chaos of a mind which aggressively seeks ever more wealth, pleasures, power, status and recognition will never find the ease and joy for which it seeks.

Dark was falling over grass and bramble. The seriousness of twilight was becoming mystery of night. A profundity beyond any possibility of measurement filled space, was space. The deer across the thicket felt it too. Being's eyes in human and deer met and there was only seeing, silence, stillness. Neither form wished to move in the perfect fullness of relatedness. Singleness and Multiplicity met in that gaze and what was shared, the secrets, which passed unspoken, were beyond the numbers One or Two, beyond the notions virtue or evil, beyond the touch of time and space.

The Nature of Mind. Opening Statement

*The ignorant do not know that oil is the essence of the
sesame seed. Likewise, not knowing the branches of
interdependence, they cannot extract their essence. Just
so the co-emergent wisdom resides in the heart of all sentient beings yet it cannot be realized unless it is pointed
out by a lama. Pounding the shell of a sesame releases
its essence. Likewise, the meaning of suchness is revealed
by the lama's instructions. Transformed into one nature,
is the inseparability of all objects. How marvelous! How
wonderful it is to see clearly in this moment the deep
meaning for which others journey far. There is no need
for the antidote wisdom. There is no path or stage to
traverse. There is no goal to achieve.*

– Tilopa

Vast unimpeded lucid clarity; this unadulterated, unfabri-
cated, unconstructed suchness is the simple fact of What Is.
It is known by mind and body when confused conceptual
elaborations cease. Then body and mind rest within That,
rest within vastness and nothingness. A sudden loss, the unmaking and undoing of all doings, the undoing of the urge
"to be," "to do," the urge of identity. This is the great, deep
Samadhi of suchness, untouchable by any word. It is the
great death while still alive that gives birth to life abundant.
Here a literal death of "identity" takes place, there is only
mystery, untouched by the idea "is" or "is not." A perfect rest
giving birth to a billion suns.

Suddenly the lucidity and clarity inherent within the
expanse, for the expanse is not a mere nothingness but a
luminous vastness, erupts from-in-as-of expanse. The eyes
of awareness open and perceive the clear light that had been
obscured by the preoccupied fixations of confusion. This

clear light is most inexplicable, it shares in the essence's impossibility of words, it is perceived and yet it is the perceiver
… and yet there is zero notion, concept, feeling of a perceiver or of an identity. What a mystery!

And "That" spontaneously recognizes. Still, calm, empty
vastness – lucid clarity suffusing, pervading … not two.
And, spontaneous self-elaborating presencing becomes all
appearances.

Auto Commentary

This opening statement is a description of the four yogas, or Naljors, of our Dzogchen lineage Calm abiding,
bright vision, non-duality, spontaneity.* These are stages
of depth that the yogi passes through in the process of
realizing the essence, nature and energy of awareness.
There is 1. The vast empty purity of space wherein there
is perfect silence and an absence of any conceptual elaboration, thinking, structuring. 2. While rested deeply
in vast, empty purity of space, there is a sudden leaping
forth of the inherent clear-light luminosity that pervades
expanse. 3. Gnostic self cognizing unborn wisdom awareness spontaneously perceives the non-duality of expanse
and luminosity. 4. Appearing and all seeming appearances
are known as the spontaneous self presencing of empty
luminous expanse wherein all of this is known as Mind's
wholeness. Mind as it is used here does not refer to the
"individual mind" with its titchy, small identity complex.
What is referred to as Mind is the wholeness of mind – its
essence, nature and energy.

* Note: Four or yogas of Dzogchen's introduction: *shi-nè (zhi gNas) /
Shamatha, lhatong (lhag mThong) / Vipashyana, nyi-mèd (nyis med) / not-
two-ness of Shamatha and Vipashyana and lhundrüp (lhun grub) / spontaneity arising from non-duality.

It is said that the nature of Mind is fundamentally made up of two aspects, *kadak* (primordial purity) and *Lhundrup* (spontaneous presencing). *Kadak* is the primordial purity aspect. *Lhundrup* is spontaneous presencing. By kadak we mean that Mind itself, in its ownmostness, is primordially pure awareness – the union of emptiness and clarity. This means that if we look at mind, we will not find anything at all and exactly this not finding is the primordially pure essence of Mind. It is kadak. The very fact of mind's emptiness – that it has no origin, no place where it abides, no place where it resolves, is purity. This is a subtle point one must relax into through meditation upon the essence.

At the same time that we do not find anything at all, or any "where" that the mind is, we discover that something is presencing. From that pure emptiness there is a self-glow, a radiance, a presencing, becoming present as in activity or a verb. In fact, in authentic Dzogchen view, communicating becomes all verbs. All appearance is the self presencing activity of unborn wisdom awareness. It is like rays of light shown through a crystal, making rainbows on the wall. There is a song prayer of Guru Rinpoche which sums up this view.

All Appearance, seen through the eyes, the universe and
    all its beings,
I see but do not take as real, I see but remain at ease and
    resting.
Dualism purified is luminous empty form appearing
Self-liberating desire, anger, precious Lama, to you I pray.
Every sound heard through the ears, whether pleasant or
    unpleasant,
I hear as sound and emptiness, free from thought's
    elaboration
Empty sound, beginningless, endless is the speech of all
    the Buddhas.

Self-liberating empty sounds, precious Lama, I pray to you.
Lotus Born Master of Oddiyana, Pema Jungne to you I pray.
Whatever thoughts move in my mind, even poisonous
  emotions,
Unaltered by anticipation, unaltered by thought's retracing,
Settling naturally in its own place, mind is free within
  the stainless.
Self-liberating pure awareness, precious Lama, to you I pray.
Lotus Born Master of Oddiyana, Pema Jungne to you I pray.
What seems to be outer, the objects to be grasped, is pure!
What seems to be inner, the mind that fixates, is empty!
What seems to lie between is luminous – may I recognize it
Joyful Buddhas of three times, look to me with compassion!
Bless beings such as me with liberation!

So in a table it is awareness tabling and in a duck it is
awareness ducking and in a human being it is awareness
humaning. There is a single ground of primordial awareness.
Primordial awareness is like gold that can be fashioned into
many items but is always still gold. The essence of awareness
is pervaded by its luminous nature, and the union of the
two of these is constantly birthing appearances – like waves
rising and falling on the ocean's surface.

If we look into mind during meditation we will only
find emptiness. If we rest in this emptiness, free from all
conceptual elaboration, we discover a spontaneous luminous pervasion. If one remains with this luminosity one
will understand appearing and appearances as the play of
luminosity within the unimpeded expanse. And if one looks
at the unimpeded purity of emptiness, one will suddenly
and spontaneously find the presencing of luminosity. Over
time, when we train mind in this fashion, appearances,
instead of seeming to imply separation, duality, birth and
death, will only point out playful presencing and all appearances as waves rising and falling. This understanding is the

realization of the nature of Mind.

The nature of Mind is not a thing. It is the dynamic interaction between spontaneous presencing and primordial purity. In Tantra and Dzogchen we call primordial purity the "All Good Mother, Kuntuzangmo." The radiance of awareness within the expanse of the Mother is the "All Good Father, Kuntuzangpo." The two of these in perfect union are the nature of Mind. One of the many reason for this symbolic presentation as All Good Father and All Good Mother is that it brings home the point that this is not an abstract concept. It is about us, in our humanness. Right here, right now.

In Mahayana, this perfect union is called *sujata garba* or *tathagata garba*. In Vajrayana it is called Buddha Nature. In Dzogchen, it is referred to as the nature of mind and the nature of awareness. These are all the same thing. If we speak in Tantric lingo, we have Dharmakaya, Sambhogakaya, and Nirmanakaya. In Dzogchen lingo, we say the essence, nature, and energy or the nature of mind. In symbolic language there is Kuntuzangmo and Kuntuzangpo and their luminous child, the magical nature of appearing.

Why, according to Dzogchen, do deluded appearances arise? They arise because Mind is unimpeded. It is the unimpeded union of emptiness and clarity, which gives rise to appearances. The nature of Mind is purely creative. Its creative thrust is beyond notions of good or bad. From the point of view of the moon, the moon is always full. From the point of view of Kuntuzangpo, appearances are always wisdom. Because Mind is unimpeded, anything and everything can arise and does arise. From the One Ground of wisdom awareness, there arise two possible paths and results.

This One Ground, the union of emptiness and clarity, has two possible vectors. At the moment when its luminous nature surges forth within-from-as-of the empty expanse – and that is every moment – there are two possibilities. With the first vector there is awareness and luminous appearing known as the play of light, intersecting, cavorting and frolicking. If the awareness aspect knows that the appearing aspects are nothing other than its own play, its own potency, its own energy, then there is natural delight. But the second vector is also a possibility in each moment. If the knowingness aspect mistakes itself for a subjective entity and mistakes the frolic of light for objective entities, it immediately becomes trapped in a ceaseless confusion of its own making, like a dream character trapped within a dream. So, One Ground – primordial awareness can lead to two paths, one that results in understanding about the actual nature of "things" and appearances, and the other resulting in confusion and a mistaken view of appearances. The two results are the joy and freedom of unborn and undying wisdom awareness' overflowing display of bliss and the sense of being trapped in bodies and realms, worlds, being, becoming, objects, relations and things.

Mythopoetic Interlude from the Tantras

Once upon a time that wasn't any kind of time at all, in a mysterious non-dimensionality of mysterious expanse, there lived an All Good King. This King was magnificent, blazing Bright Virtue. He wore the whole of the sky as a garment, a cloak of the stars and a belt made from the planets strung like pearls. In his right hand he held the sun and in his left he held the moon. Free from every constraint, his very perception gave rise to ceaseless appearances of beauty and splendor. He was indeed the All Good Father of everything.

At this time there was also an Auspicious Queen. The mystery of her love was such that no idea, word, concept could reach its heights or plumb its depths. Because no word could encompass the mystery of her, she had many names. She was called All Good Mother for she was the womb space of all appearing. She was called Auspicious Queen because from her depths only goodness is given birth. She is called Birthplace and Charnel Ground, for she is the birthplace of Buddhas and sentient beings and where they resolve in death. From her, Buddhas and beings are born and yet there is never any increase in Buddhas and beings. In her, Buddhas and beings perish and yet there is no loss.

This All Good Queen of the expanse and the All Good King of luminosity were full of love and joy. They cavorted in, and as, the perfect union of expanse and light without even the notion self or other, with no notion of two beings or of union. Their closeness was beyond the concepts separation or togetherness … they were not two, they were not One, they were beyond enumeration in their mutuality and love. And, as love play tends to do, they gave birth to a child, a son. That which is without origin or birth is birthed from the birthless without ever having been born. It is the truest mystery of incarnation and appearance. And the son had a name, Luminous Blazing.

This child was made of play-full-ness, as all children are. He had no fear, for all appearances were not other than his home, his family, his parents, himself. He went out venturing across the ends of space, creating space as he went. He went exploring in all manner of countless, infinite appearances. He journeyed through all possible configurations of the shattering of light in joy. In all of this exploration, in all of this wandering about, he was utterly fearless because he had no notion of subject or object, internal or external, here or there, self or other. This is what allowed him to be so playful in his adventures.

And so, as must happen in all fairy tales – because they speak the truth of Beingness – in the midst of all this ad-venturing, without cause or reason, he found himself one day in a dark and murky place. He found himself suddenly ensconced in an endarkened realm. He wasn't avoiding it and he wasn't looking for it, he suddenly was just there. And in this endarkenment he found himself suddenly to exist, found himself to be a separate being in an actual place, time and dimension. Suddenly, confused to find himself to exist as some this or that, he found himself in a dilemma. He did not know what he was, where he was, how he was. He did not know if he would endure, perish, fail or succeed, and all of these, in and of themselves, were the very description of the realm in which he found himself, called a self.

He had ventured fearlessly into all experiences and so now he was within new experiences which included fear, birth, death, gain, loss, shame, fame and the sensation of suf-fering and stuckness. He began to seek and he began to seek in the only place he was – the realm of endarkenment. But as the realm itself was the shape of his endarkening, there was no solution to be found within the confines if its paradoxical axioms. For lifetimes and lifetimes, as all manner of being, he lived in this realm. He sought happiness in pleasures, power, relationships, here and there looking for some sign of the ease he still intuited from his former life.

Now his All Good Father and Mother, Kuntuzangpo and Kuntuzangmo, having uncontrived, spontaneous, great natural compassion as the energy of their mysterious appearance-nonexistence, felt sympathy for their child. They could feel his frantic panic, for it was not taking place in any place other than the place that they always already were and in truth he was only lost in hallucinations. He was right there always already with them, as them, of them. They called out to him again and again but all he would hear were faint strains of some unknowable, beautiful music. They would manifest to him in the guises of his realm as a passing sage, a Bodhisattva animal, the enbrightening of dawn sunlight but he was unable to understand their symbolic presentation in the midst of his endarkened fears. He did, however, feel their communication as an ever-growing longing within his heart, body, mind and being, a longing for an unknown freedom, an unknown happiness that had no seeds of falling back into suffering. He felt he needed to return home.

And so this motivated him, moved him, pushed him in his search. All the appearances that before had neither existence nor nonexistence now were concrete existence. All the spaces, which before were simply luminous radiance, neither empty nor full, were now realms of beings. He began to explore in all these different realms of being. He began to look into things for some intuition, some sparkling through or whispering of the mystery he longed for. He sought happiness and gradually came to understand that true happiness could not come from things that change. The happiness he sought, he remembered vaguely, was a perfect freedom from suffering. And so he involved himself in spiritual pursuits of a more subtle nature and his ability or his capacity to discern the subtle meaning of symbols and whisperings in his ear became more acute. Finally he could begin to understand the meaning of symbols, whispers and indications until one day he recognized an emanation of the All Good Mother who was named Pregnant Raincloud and he listened with great care to her instructions.

She spoke of mysterious things, of a gem whose qualities were so astounding and amazing that it was called the Wish Fulfilling Jewel. Whatever pure intentions or wishes were formulated by one who had this luminously blazing jewel would naturally and spontaneously come to pass. She said the jewel was owned by an old blind woman who was known only as Blind Grandmother, and that she lived in an octagonal palace made of magic that could only be approached by five horsemen, five warriors. Luminous Blazing must travel with the five warriors to where they would free five prisoners. These prisoners held the secret of the Wish Fulfilling Jewel's location.

Many adventures come to pass as Luminous Blazing seeks out the five warriors. Finally the little child finds himself in the palace of the Blind Grandmother. The palace is filled to overflowing with children, servants and warriors. At the center of the palace is the Blind Grandmother holding the Wish Fulfilling Jewel. Whenever he looks at it, it is a different color; it sparkles and shimmers in five colors. It is never the same color and most mysteriously, when he looks at it directly, it has no color whatsoever. The Blind Grandmother is laughing, telling him that there is no chance he can ever have this jewel. That there is no way anyone can get this jewel.

Having become quite sensitive, Luminous Blazing also begins to hear the words of his own All Good Mother in his ear. She is saying, "Do not believe her. Ask what the price is and when she says no one will pay it say, 'Then I will be that no one!'" The child does this and the startled Blind Grandmother reluctantly says, "There are eight payments to be made." 1. The price is the price of all one's intellectual conceit – one has to pay that price. One has to give up every concept of what is known and unknown. 2. One has to give up the arrogance of subjectivity and objectivity. 3. One has to give all the grasping of a mountain of desire. 4. One has to give all of the striving and work that has been done throughout the ages. 5. The conceit of self-concern. 6. The conceit of attainment. 7. One must pay with the conceit of enlightenment. 8. One must pay with the conceit of Being.

Now the little child's living is running toward his loving shouting, "What a bargain! I'll buy it!" And in that moment he awakens from his dreaming of darkness and suffering. In that moment he does not find himself anywhere but in the only place he ever had been. In that moment he does not find himself somehow different, greater, stronger, more famous or more powerful . . . in fact he does not find his "self" at all but again recognizes the play of knowing and luminosity as the only game in town. Now mother, father, child and all appearing are what they have always been.

What sees from the eyes is utter emptiness? No self. Expanse without explanation. For "that" even the arising and extinction of the universe is a matter of no import or implication at all. Because of this appearances become a playground.

∽

The sage has no fearlessness because they have no fear. They have no death because they have given up the lie of birth. They have no insecurity because they have no security. They have no "other" because they have no self. They have no consciousness because they have no unconsciousness.

∽

Buddhas and sentient beings, these two concepts are such utter rubbish. Once you have admitted to the lie of birth and death, you will have to deal with such rubbish. In that I have no interest.

∽

A school does not take advantage of the superstitions existing commonly among men, nor does it play on the fears and beliefs surrounding survival. It does not trade services for material considerations and its teaching cannot be bought at any price. It remains neither hidden or exposed, neither available to the general public nor unreachable by those in need of a school. It is an entity existing unto itself . . .
– E. J. Gold, from *The Joy of Sacrifice*, 16, 19

∽

Stages of Unknowing

The contemplative process moves through stages of unknowing into perfect annihilation of knowing. It is only in the perfection of unknowing that the illumination of wisdom might dawn. One might say that the perfection of wisdom is perfect unknowing, revealing a luminous ignorance.

Mind, with all its surety and anxiety, is made up of its knowings. It is made up of its knowledge. This knowledge is always a collection of bits and pieces from the past arranged as curios in the entry hall of mind. In the beginning, people tend to think that spiritual life is a glorious quest for new bits and pieces of especially arcane and interesting knowledge and, certainly, that does seem to come with the territory. But is not the point. Rather it is a byproduct.

Knowing solidifies into the rigidity of unquestioned superstition. Some of these superstitions are taken as so self-obvious that they are next to impossible to question. Once this was true of the fact that "the world is flat" or that "the earth is the center of the solar system." Like these two erroneous conclusions, the superstition that anything like birth or death ever happened to any person is another absurd falsity that is almost unquestionable to most people.

When the tangled mess of concepts that make up most people's world-view is unraveled there is less and less to know. Spiritual life matures in a deep silence whose quietude is wisdom and whose extent is prayer. Within this unmaking of knowledge there is a tremendous release of energy which, when set free from erroneous constructs, turns out to be something quite unspeakable and utterly divine. It also turns out to be the substanceless substance of everything and every thing.

First one must enter the cavern of unknowing where all created objects and concepts – including self, god, being, enlightenment, bondage, wisdom, ignorance are lost. It is only when there is a tremendous courage, through which one rests in and is then dissolved in, this dark emptiness that natural great awareness' suprasensual luminosity comes to be known ... but it is only known in an absolute help-lessness, for there is no self to "help," no god, no guru, no Buddha, no "other" to help the self that is not there anymore. It is a flight of the alone to the alone.

In that moment of darkness and helplessness, and only there, it can happen that awareness, devoid of any sense of self or object – experience or experiencer – discovers that emptiness is not a mere nothingness but an expanse replete with potential qualities. In that moment, one discovers that the luminous expanse of nothingness is the birthplace and homeland of joy, fearlessness, wisdom and compassion.

This can be thought about or spoken about with lan-guage and concept but it cannot be known that way. In the first unknowing one will loses everything ... religion, home-land, self, even Being ... every word, every concept is lost ... forever. In the subsequent knowing there is no concretizing into knowledge but only an unutterable mystery that divulg-es itself in every and all appearing.

After the dark of unknowing and the bright of luminous ignorance there is no chance any longer for narrow dogma based on word, ideology, attachment to this or that tradition or country. Body then lives as space's joy, free from threat of terrorists, free from territory to defend.

∾

A friend from Greece wrote: "And what is your take on Origen's view of apokatastasis that the church later declared heresy?" I replied, "A man fell deeply into sleep wherein he dreamt that his leg was mangled by a car. In the dream he suffered terribly. Upon waking, he was overjoyed to discover his leg whole and healthy and declared, "Praise be to the reconstitution of my leg!" … and thus one might understand apokatastasis – reconstitution, restoration to the original primordial condition … Perhaps some wake from the dream and yet other dream characters go on dreaming. For them the leg is mangled … and this Gnostic knowing is heresy. Wisdom will always be heresy to the unwise. Compassion is then the spontaneous response of wisdom to dreaming's suffering.

It is, however, good to remember that if you take the false away from those uninterested in the real, you only succeed in making them doubly homeless – and that is mean."

In Conversation with a Young Dakini

I said, "A geography of love is an impossibility."
She said, "Why is it impossible?"
I replied, "Because from beginningless non-time there
has never been the slightest atom of actual substance
material phenomena which could become mountain and
valley."
She laughed and answered back, "And yet, empty
appearance appearing cares not one whit. Fertile valleys,
impossibly high mountains, the expanse of stars all right
here, my love."

I am conquered by her logic. Evening falls and whole gardens of night blooming flowers open to release nectar to this drunken night bee. If I was a theologian or philosopher I might fret over impossibilities but the sage is a lover who cavorts free and easy in the dream boudoir of appearance.

In the geography of immediacy mind travels. The mist moved drunkenly through the forest – slow, sensuously drifting, winding. Mind travels as trees, like shrouded figures, creaking in a wind. In twilight everyplace became the someplace of mystery where mind travels.

This mind of traveling, a radiance subsumed in mystery, winds sensuously without words, without thought, without self, without other. It winds through appearing untouched and yet intimate – free, recognizing appearances as its own play. Mind's traveling, when lost in confusion, wanders the shrouded corridors of experience startling at phantasms and projections.

Hard edges of righteous wrongness lose their tight angles in silent love's twilight. Thinking rested in silence becomes flickers of brightness. Sense of depth and distinction frolic and tumble in the opacity of confusion's evening as whole vistas of wonderment open outward.

A large tree that had been hit by lightening the previous year, its rotting and charred trunk now home to bugs, birds, squirrels and more, became in this gloaming hour a shadow play of dark and white. The body perfectly still, mind utterly silent, stood transfixed, looking and looking at the changes of misty pattern across its wide form. Suddenly an owl burst forth from a hole high up in the trunk with a screech. Without thought, without emotive content, the body-mind-feeling-wholeness burst out laughing with unbearable fullness.

Go out into the woods. Go out where no one can see and pour your heart out to divine mystery. Let mind flow out from mind until silence sublimes. Let thought's confused insistence slip from tongue and lip until silence settles. Then true prayer awakens. True prayer, found in the sense field's perfect brightness, held in mind's silence, pervades and is pervaded by unimaginable godliness ...

When this is known then all of nature becomes the symbolic divulgence of perfect freedom, joy and love. When this has become unchanging, then one's life has become symbol and divulgence as well.

Concepts create idols; only wonder comprehends anything. People kill one another over idols. Wonder makes us fall to our knees.

– St. Gregory of Nyssa

A Universe of Light

Imagine a universe comprised entirely of light. There is nothing but light. No things, just light. An expanse of light with no objects. Imagine somehow you are standing in a space outside of this universe of light looking at it. What would you see? Would you see a great brightness? Would you see expansive luminosity? No. You wouldn't see anything at all. You would just see clear through it like a clear pane of glass. You would see nothing because you cannot see clear light. You only know light when it hits an object and you see the reflective glow.

Next, imagine you pick up a salt shaker and toss it into the universe of light. What would happen? Two things. The salt shaker would be brightly illuminated from every angle and side. Secondarily and simultaneously, you would know that the universe was suffused by light. You would know this by the reflection of light bouncing off an object. The potential to illuminate would have always been there but it would be latent and not actualized because there was no secondary circumstance contributing to knowing the light's illuminating capacity. The light would still have been present but what lets us know light, its illuminating nature, would have been unactualized.

Now imagine a universe made entirely of knowingness, awareness, only awareness with no objects. Would the awareness be aware of itself? No. Awareness is like the light. It remains latent until its nature is actualized. The nature of awareness is its luminous knowingness, its capacity to know. Until the salt shaker was thrown into the light, if it had the capacity for knowingness, it would have remained unaware of its own illuminating nature. Until you throw that salt shaker into the universe of awareness, it would remain unaware of its own capacity for knowingness. Throw the salt shaker in and suddenly the universe knows two things: 1. the salt shaker, and 2. its own capacity for knowingness.

We live in a universe made entirely of luminous awareness. The essence of this awareness is a mystery, unutterable because it is prior even to the salt shaker. It is the deep mystery wherefrom knowingness emerges as an object appears. The universe we live in is made of luminous awareness and one aspect is the knowingness and the other aspect is the luminous playful display. The luminous aspect is always displaying itself in all manner of showmanship. My Guru used to say, "Appearance is the outrageous flirtatiousness of Being."

There is a moment, and it is every moment, when the self-luminous glow of awareness is emerging from the essence of mystery. In that moment, if the self-luminous glow of awareness recognizes itself as the play of mystery and also recognizes appearances as the same play, then no problem can ever arise. Then everything is known as temporary, unnecessary, modification of unborn wisdom light. Awareness flirts with itself as appearance. Appearance allows itself to be ceaselessly seduced by expanse. The wave rises, falls, rises again. Same ocean.

In every moment, emptiness, the expanse of perfect mystery is giving itself away in a wild reckless love affair with appearing. It throws emptiness aside into somethingness, it flows out from itself without any thought of self, and in becoming somethingness even seems to die into its love. And every moment, somethingness is dissolving, resolving, surrendering into emptiness, into expanse. Wave rises, wave falls, rises again. Same ocean. This giving of oneself, this surrender, this wild love, is the context of appearing and so it also characterizes the content of appearing.

Confused beings, not knowing, not seeing, not living this process of surrender, try to latch onto some small piece of appearing – a birth, a life, experiences – and because nothing can be grasped, everything is impermanent, a modification of light, they cause themselves great suffering. The sage abides as the tidal motion of emptiness and somethingness, of expanse and luminosity and rides the ever-shifting changes as love. It's that simple. As love. My Guru said to me, "Nirmanakaya is love." And it is. It is love swinging on the love swing of emptiness and somethingness.

PART II
LETTERS
TO FRIENDS

I have returned to my village after twenty years;
No sign of old friends or relatives – they have all died
    or gone away.
My dreams are shattered by the sound of the temple bell
    struck at sunrise.
An empty floor, no shadows; the light has long been
    extinguished.

– Ryokan, *One Robe One Bowl*, 39

Dear Friend,

You ask me, "What is this world?" It is union. It is *rasa*, the flavor of feeling that is love play. Wave meets shore, the edge where ice melt becomes water, where twilight meets nightfall, one body meets another, one delicate indeterminacy called human being meets another, sight meets object of the eye, hand meets stairway railing. This world is the child of blissful union between mystery's vast expanse and luminous clarity's playfulness. Born of love play, its every moment is the emblem of union, the symbol of union's secret liberation possibility!

Now you know me and you know I am not a new Age Soft Core Porn enthusiast. But, at the same time, I am endlessly surprised by how numb your standard Protestant Westerner, who carries original sin mentality down into the deepest aspects of their lives, is unaffected or never questions why we spend our days meditating on couples having sex. The whole of Tantra's teachings deal with human beings on a human level, and human beings are fixated on desire and aggression. And so Tantra uses desire and aggression as alchemical agents of transformation. Starting with refuge and the image of Orgyan Dorje Chang, on to Vajrasattva Yabyum right on up to Guru Yoga we meditate on union and on the symbolic and alchemical meaning of the energy inherent in the felt images and imaged feelings of sexuality. Why? Because this world is made of that – literally. This world is molded from desire and it is in the understanding of desire that we will find its origin and meaning.

This world is Tulku. You may know this Tibetan word for a reincarnated Tantric teacher. "So and so is the tulku of so and so." In this sense it has been degraded so deeply that it may well be the end of Vajrayana. It has turned the radical nature of Vajrayana into medieval church politics.

But then it is surprising how many great great grandchildren of the Reformation secretly want the Pope back in their lives, secretly long for the abnegation of authority that comes with unthinking religious fixations. But Tulku means Nirmanakaya, it means the appearance of wisdom bliss, Buddha nature, in the world of appearing. Those with wisdom understand that there is only one true Tulku and that is all of appearance. The body of appearance arising from empty clarity is Tulku. It is the appearance of godliness, the divine, Buddha Nature and in the words of my Guru it is the appearance of Love.

Where there is the will to power, there is no love and where there is love there is no will to power. Love is the only sign of realization. In this realm all that is good is related to Union. Love wed to wisdom gives birth to compassion. The word for compassion in Dzogchen terminology is also the word for the energy of appearance. So, what I am saying is appearance itself is the only true Tulku – Nirmanakaya, one of the three bodies of the Buddha's reality. There is the Dharmakaya, the emblem of Buddha's mind that is the vast open aspect. Buddha's mind free of all possible definitions of pure mystery beyond conceptuality and language. There is a Sambhogakaya, which is the radiance of that mystery and open luminous clarity filled with infinite qualities of wisdom bliss. A dense array of wisdom bliss. And the union of these two gives birth to the Nirmanakaya – a ceaseless magical manifestation of luminous wisdom bliss as the endless modifications of light appearing as all appearances. When the empty essence and the luminous clarity bed down together (and they always are – what lushes!), it is their union of bliss emptiness that produces its orgasmic delight. The result is the magical child of illusion called appearance, the acting force of wisdom bliss. It is dynamic and active. It is not passive. Wisdom is not passive and aloof.

There is a tendency in modern Western culture to portray Christ in books and movies as a kind of idiot savant or as a sort of a whining mama's boy, but wisdom is not passive or retarded in some fashion. Wisdom is dynamic and active. It is active in, and even as, all appearance. It is possible therefore for the thread of compassion to become so finely trained that it can manifest again and again in the realm of being as a particular line of incarnation, so this also would be Tulku.

Tulku is not status but only function, the function of love. Guru is not status. It is function. There is no question that it would be best if all power, authority, wealth, politics, could be stripped from religion and spirituality. If there was nothing for ego to gain and only the function of love in the service of beings, then there would be no impetus for ego to build monuments from spiritual life. Tulkus as this or that person is the relative and minor aspect of the meaning of Tulku. But the deeper and real meaning of the word refers to the nature of appearance itself. When mind gives up delusion and dissolves in the pure mystery beyond being or even awareness, then one recognizes appearance, recognizes (the prefix re- meaning "again," and cognize "to know"), one knows appearance again in a new way when seeing appearance as it truly is, as it is in its simple direct straight forward presentation of wisdom bliss. The essence of awareness is open space, the nature is luminous bliss, and these two frolic and play together in inseparable love. The rasa, the shimmering feeling taste, of their play shimmers as all worlds. The whole world is the incarnation of wisdom bliss.

When awareness becomes confused, becomes deluded consciousness, seeming to abide as the limit of a single body, single lifetime, set of experiences, there is suffering. Even in this state the reality of appearance and the *kayas* continually act as a self-liberating dynamic within the form and flesh of all appearance. The self-liberating dynamic of enlightenment appears in the worlds as gurus, lamas, lineage, and tulkus to serve of-as-from-in love to the world. They serve as reminder that love, not power, is the doorway to truth.

So "What is the world?" It is the single appearance of love bliss; that is what it is. Tantra does not fight with what you are, and you are the result of and desire for union. At the relative level you are the union of your parents, at the subtle level you are the union of awareness and perception, at the original level you are the union of emptiness and clarity. You seek union, desire union, in sex, in wanting a nice shirt, or car, good job, friends... everything you desire because you are MADE FROM THE URGE TOWARD UNION. Desire is not the problem. Desire misunderstood is the problem. Mistaking what is inner for what is outer creates the problem of desire. All external desires are symbols of what you long for internally. The wholeness you wish for, union with no separation, is found within the construct of awareness you call body. When you discover this you will be the master of desire and a being of wisdom.

With affection,
        This mangy dog, Traktung

you poor sad thing thinking death is real
all by itself
        – Ikkyū, *Crow With No Mouth: 15th Century*
        Zen Master. Versions by Stephen Berg.

Dear Friend,

You follow up you last question with "What is desire?" This
is a very good question, and so I will tell you a little mythopoetic psychocosmology from the Tantras. In the practices
of Tummo (Tantric practice of Inner Heat and bliss) there is
an "A" syllable visualized in the navel and a "HAM" syllable
visualized in the head. Well, in the practice the A and the HAM
really wish, long for, DESIRE to get back together. The whole
practice is about working with the subtle body's channels and
winds (*nadi/prana, tsa/lung*) so that these two drops (*bindu,ti-
gle*) can get back together. It is said in Tantra that every bit
of desire a human being feels is a reflection of the desire that
these two *bindu* within the subtle body have for each other.

Okay, here is how a human being comes about. In the
beginning there was a single great indestructible drop. This
drop is known by many names, Sugatagarbha, Buddha
Nature, Enlightenment, Prajnaparamita, Dzogchen,
Mahamudra, Mystery, Self, Wisdom Bliss… the list goes on
and on. In its play-full-ness this drop seemed to divide into
two, a red drop and a white drop. Really the two never left
the wholeness of wholeness but playfulness is playfulness
and so there ensued a massive psychodrama of twoness and
all the possibilities of twoness. The white drop went up and
the red drop descended and in this motion, up and down,
ascent and descent came into being, dimensionality came
into being and the subtle central channel of the yogic body
was the thread between the two. The white drop ascended
to the space that becomes the head and the red drop to the
space slightly below the navel in the human body. The body
then grows on this axis.

The white drop has the nature of the syllable HAM and
the red drop has the nature of the syllable A. Why are these
A and HAM? Because A and HAM together make AHAM, the

word for "I" the feeling of Beingness. "A" is the luminous appearing aspect of Beingness and HAM is the knowingness aspect. "A" is the female aspect and HAM the male aspect. Sometimes people ask, "Why is the female aspect the appearance aspect? I thought femaleness in Buddhism was emptiness?" Yes, that is right, and here it is being emphasized that appearances *are* emptiness! As it says in the *Prajnaparamita Sutras*, "Here O Shariputra, form is emptiness and emptiness is form. Form is not other than emptiness and emptiness is not other than form." So the glow of Beingness becomes beings in worlds. The knowingness becomes a subjective knower and the luminous glow becomes the play of appearances. Then the A and the HAM, the subjective and the appearing aspects are separated – in the whole and in the human body ... as without so within. They want very very much to get back together.

The moment the self-luminous glow of awareness surges forth from the empty expanse of mystery (and that is every moment) there is the possibility of wisdom or confusion. If there is wisdom then subject and object never become two. They are also not One. They are beyond all such enumeration. They abide as the paradox of wisdom bliss' empty appearing. If the self-glow mistakes itself for a subjective entity and the luminous frolic as external appearances, then there is duality. In that moment, being clothes itself as a particular being in a realm, a world. We are Being clothed as human beings in the human realm. The longing of the A and the HAM to reunite is born as desire within us. The longing of Beingness to subsume itself in the mystery beyond Being, to liberate itself from sudden confusion is felt as all desires within us. In the beginning we do not hear the longing with clarity and so we confuse it as this and that desire. But we can mature in terms of our desiring.

Children tend to desire security and objects, teens desire pleasure and love, adults desire love and compassion.

We grow and move through stages of desiring – unless we become stuck at one or another immature stage. All desire is nothing but the red and white drops wishing to have union. When we meditate on the four joys of Tummo and Karmamudra (sexual yogas) we are refining the union of bliss and emptiness, which results in the most profound understanding of desire and its implications. In the progressive experience of the four joys there is ever more pleasure and sense of union until finally, in the fourth joy, there is union beyond all separation. This is called "beyond joy," because it is beyond all words and concepts. In the slippery wet edge between third and fourth joy one feels the glow of Being.

When you practice Tummo or Karmamudra you are going to the edge of Beingness where the first mistake of duality was made, to the place where luminous mystery became AHAM and then split into A and HAM, giving birth to realms and worlds. Beingness has split itself into A and HAM. "A" is the very essence, the red fiery essence, which becomes all aspects of the red drop in appearance. HAM is the liquid mercury purity of the white drop of all aspects of knowingness, confused or Gnostic.

"A" and HAM became the two mandalas, the mandala of what is grasped and the mandala of what fixates. What is grasped is appearances, and what fixates is thought. The mandala of what is grasped is all appearance arising from the red drop – intrinsically pure and empty. But fixation of the mind makes appearances seem solid, just as things in a dream appear solid due to mind's fixation during sleep. The A becomes appearance and the HAM, confusing appearances as external, fixates on them with attraction, aversion or indifference never realizing that they are only the projection of this imagined separation. Each being then develops their own forms of seeking without for what can only be satisfied within. The A and HAM are always looking for each other in all appearances,

boys and girls, men and women, dogs, cats, carpets, dia-
monds, cars, power, status, relationship and everything else.

In Tummo and Karmamudra practice, we bring these
two drops together. The A and HAM are introduced to each
other and we bring them together to know great wisdom.
It is Guru Rinpoche's dating service! At this point, you will
thank me for having taught you to sit without slouching
because it is the body's strong and pure posture that facili-
tates the movement of wisdom winds in the channels. The
channels are not dependent on the body; the body is dependent on the channels – but, at the same time, one's posture
also affects one's mind. At a certain point any concern with
posture is irrelevant but that is later when you have realized
luminous emptiness prior to appearances.

So this is a little bit about desire and how it arises. I hope
it makes sense in relation to the practices you are doing. In
the end one discovers all words fall short. And yet, words
are needed to communicate. What is important is to look
into the deep meaning of the words, their implications and
consider the implications in your life.

With great aimless affection,

t.

Unite male and female energies developing the method
of mixing higher and lower energies, female assisting
male and male assisting female, the principle of each
being separately practiced. Intensify and elevate your
practice, broadening the horizons of your pleasure; but
if pleasure and Emptiness are not identified, pointlessly
you stray from the path of Tantra: apprehend the intrinsic unity of pleasure and Emptiness.
    – Yeshe Tsogyel, Sky Dancer, Keith Dowman

Dearest Friend,

You ask how to reconcile the demands of the path and the constraints of *samaya* (vows) with Dzogchen's call for spontaneity. The 19th-century writer John Jay Chapman once said of politicians "that when forced to decide between lucrative malpractice and thankless honesty they usually chose the first." In response to your question: certainly it would be easier, and more pleasing to us both, to simply tell you what you wish to hear! I myself am merely a politician offering disciples false security and sham superiority in exchange for comfort and status. Still somehow the Buddha's wisdom teachings manage to affect my hard hide mind, and I find myself compelled to answer truthfully,

You seem concerned that mindfulness, in regards to respect, considerations of others, compassion and the like, will cause you to become stilted and "lose your Dzogchen sense of uncontrived ease." I suddenly find myself laughing as I remember that once, when asked about why we are embarrassed by our faith and devotion and tend to hide it around others, Thinley Norbu Rinpoche replied, "How can you hide what you do not have?" So now I say to you, "How can you lose what you do not have?"

In the Khyentse Yeshe Dorje's commentary on confession practice called "Stainless Crystal" it says, "Even though no flaw or habit has touched unconditioned natural awareness we yogins ensnared by seemingly dualistic phenomena must follow the path." Until such time as mental fabrication's very last restrictive habit is severed we must practice to purify *samsara*'s temporary ignorance, its insistence that spiritual results can be had with little or no effort. You are confusing spontaneity with the comfort of indulging our personality-driven habits whose function it is to maintain the separative sense of self. To follow in the groove of repetitive patterns takes little effort, should not be confused with the uncontrived spontaneity of authentic Dzogpa Chenpo. This style of relaxed "spontaneity" is like teenagers who enjoy playing at being grown up so long as their parents pay all the bills. Parents' demands to increasingly take responsibility for oneself seem oppressive to a teenager, but they are in fact merely an introduction to what adult life requires in order for the child to achieve authentic independence.

If we have a habit, and we simply indulge this habit, this "feels natural." The force of our habits spontaneously flows from the interaction of afflictive mind stirring the all ground consciousness. If we blindly follow these habits we will not feel contrived or stilted but we will also never escape suffering. Why is this? Our lives, with their birth, sickness, old age and death, are nothing other than this repetitive process whose name is samsara unless we discover freedom through disciplined practice. To relax into samsara's habit, samsara's self-elaborating display always tinged by suffering, is not the practice of a Dzogchenpa! In *White Sail*'s chapter "Cleaning Deviations," Thinley Norbu Rinpoche writes,

> The teachings of Buddhism reveal that mind is the basis of the infinite variations of phenomena, encouraging us to influence our own phenomena so that we can try to create positive energy through positive intention in order to go beyond our habits and recognize natural awareness.

We practice so that non-virtue habit becomes virtue habit in order to go beyond all habit. What you are complaining about is the work necessary to counteract non-virtue habit. In other words you are saying that the accumulation of merit is tedious and you would prefer to simply call non-virtue "Dzogchen spontaneity."

In fresh natural mind's stainless open space not only do habits not exist, but even the essence of mind cannot be said to exist. It is only in this context of primordial purity's spontaneous presencing, outside the stain of habit, that we can speak of true uncontrived spontaneity. What is called "uncontrived" from the point of view of samsara is merely following after samsara's temporary habit patterns without mindfulness. This is like a moth, out of its natural spontaneous love of light, flying into a candle flame.

Where no effort at mindfulness is made, habit's unrelenting flow is felt to be "spontaneous." Because you have become accustomed to your habits they feel "natural." Because you don't have to be mindful in order to follow habit's dictates you call such behavior "uncontrived." Because it seems "spontaneous" and "uncontrived" you think it is the great ease of a Dzogchen. Resting in samsara's variegated habit patterning you attempt to cover over shabby behavior, arisen from habit, behind the words "spontaneous" or "uncontrived."

Nestling in shit is the "spontaneous" behavior of dung beetles in accord with "uncontrived" dung loving habit.

Wallowing in filth is the "spontaneous" behavior of pigs in accord with "uncontrived" inability to sweat habit.

Miserliness is the "spontaneous" behavior of rich people in accord with "uncontrived" impermanence's anxiety habit.

Violent beatings are the "spontaneous" behavior of abusive people in accord with anger's "uncontrived" fearfulness habit.

Cheating on wives is the "spontaneous" behavior of

wandering husbands in accord with lust's "uncontrived" hard cock habit.

Yelling and screaming is the "spontaneous" behavior of wives in accord with jealousy's "uncontrived" territoriality habit.

Not understanding the teachings, no matter how often they are repeated, is the "spontaneous" behavior of some students in accord with ignorance's "uncontrived" stupidity habit.

Low slung jeans are the "spontaneous" behavior of teen-age girls in accord with flirtation's "uncontrived" spider and fly habit.

Secret glances are the "spontaneous" behavior of monks in accord with sexual frustration's "uncontrived" volcano habit.

Shamelessness is the "spontaneous" behavior of some Tantricas in accord with debauchery's "uncontrived" promiscuity habit.

Rolls Royces and silver tea sets are the "spontaneous" behavior of fancy pants Gurus in accord with pompousness' "uncontrived" vanity habit.

Ass kissing is the "spontaneous" behavior of sycophantic disciples in accord with self-seeking's "uncontrived" personal advantage habit.

Lack of respect is the "spontaneous" behavior of pseudo Dzogchenpas in accord with arrogance's "uncontrived" overbearing pride habit.

In *Magic Dance,* Thinley Norbu Rinpoche says, *"Even if we only have one conception left, only one phenomena, whether good or bad, it is still residual habit which obscures."* Buddhists transform gross unvirtuous habits into virtue habit in order to go beyond all habit. In this way we discover the stainless sky of wisdom mind's empty luminous space. Certainly, when we are under habit's tyranny, it feels more natural and easeful to simply go along. If we shun mindfulness, so that we do not even recognize habit as habit, then habit will seem like spontaneity! This, however, is like a drowning man who simply relaxes and sinks to the bottom to die or like a concentration camp victim who befriends the guards to win greater comforts. The result is only suffering for oneself and others. All the varying paths and schools of Buddhism teach that mind must be purified of habit's stranglehold. Nowhere will you find any teaching suggesting that blindly following dualistic habit is the same as the uncontrived jewel-like activity of the Buddha.

Changing habit is always uncomfortable because habit is momentum. Ego is not a thing, it is an activity. Ego is the vectoral momentum of habit. A vector is any quantity, such as force, velocity or acceleration, which has both magnitude and direction. Buddha's wisdom mind has no direction and no substance. Sentient being's mental fabrications are the origin of direction, momentum and substance! These three are the essence of habit and their variation appears as the six realms. A vector can be symbolized by an arrow pointing in the direction of its movement. The arrow of mental fabrication's habit points toward frustration and suffering. The arrow of the Vajrayana's sublime path points toward the extinction of suffering. Buddha's directionless vector of substanceless wisdom phenomena is beyond pointing or partiality.

Because, for lifetimes, we are already moving in the direction of samsara's arrow, the momentum makes it difficult to stop. We must make an effort to be mindful and transform samsara's suffering habits into Buddha's stainless compassion. If we are traveling fast in a car and we put on the brakes suddenly we might hear screeching and smell smoke from the tires. In the same way, when we try to stop gross habits, which bring ourselves and others suffering, we will feel a dynamic tension from opposing forces. In Sanskrit this is called *tapas,* the heat generated by friction between our intention towards virtue and the habit of non-virtue. This feeling is what you are calling "contrived." The fact that it feels stilted or contrived is merely evidence that you are, as yet, unable to practice the relaxed effortless method of Dzogchen.

Dzogchen is not effortless because it simply ignores the problem of delusion's habit. In all vehicles of the Buddha's teachings from the Shravaka to Dzogpa Chenpo the problem of samsaric habit is addressed through the varying methods of renunciation, transformation and self-liberation. Dozgchen's self-liberation is not to simply give into ego's demands and indulge in every habit without mindfulness. It is, rather, the perfection of mindfulness as wisdom, the practice of never straying into habit at all! Your question reveals that this distinction between delusion and wisdom is not yet clear to you so please do not destroy further chance of learning by indulging in pseudo intellectual Dzogchen word games.

I began with a quote from John Jay Chapman and I will give you another one now, "A vision of truth which does not call upon us to get out of our armchair – why, this is the desideratum of mankind." In other words, if it is hard most people will not want to do it. We all wish to be free from demands. The Buddhist practitioner renounces samsara's demands in favor of the demands of the spiritual path because these demands lead beyond all demand into authentic freedom.

Learning to drive a car feels very unnatural and contrived at first. There are so many things to remember, and we are not born with clutch, gas and gearshift habit. After some time we develop clutch, gas and gearshift habit, and driving not only feels uncontrived but also offers us great freedom. Transforming non-virtue into virtue is much the same. The accumulation of merit brings us great freedom and joy. What in the beginning seems stilted, in the end is discovered to be natural happiness. The yogi wishes to escape samsara's oppressive environment to drive as swiftly as possible to naturally arisen wisdom playgrounds to play with sublime playmates.

So please do not take this matter lightly and call following after samsaric habits "uncontrived activity." Often what is sweet in the beginning is bitter in the end and what is bitter in the beginning is sweet in the end. Following after samsara's habit tastes sweet in the beginning but samsara's suffering is a bitter pill in the end. The path of wisdom's irritating argument with samsara may taste a little bitter in the beginning, feel a little stilted, but its deathless celestial pureland is sweet in the end. Perhaps this path is harder than learning to drive a car but the palace of uncontrived wisdom luminosity is significantly superior to the mall! Thinley Norbu Rinpoche has said it very nicely in *White Sail's* chapter on "Cleaning Deviations."

Whether one wants to make one's own phenomena into dualistic habit or the enlightened appearance of wisdom deities is not decided outwardly; it is one's own choice.

Good luck, with love,

t.

Dearest Friend of our Friend,

You ask about compassion in the non-dual state. Yes, it is intentionless. You seem a bit confused by the idea of "intentionless compassion." In the non-dual state there are no contrived actions at all. The word in Tibetan is *trinle*, spontaneous activity of a sort that is always a perfect responsiveness to any situation. Because it arises from the expanse of luminous virtue qualities it always has the character of wisdom, compassion, beauty, truth and goodness. This is difficult to understand because right now you struggle to manifest virtue when negative habits override. And also because when we conceptually consider dharma teachings that we are not yet capable of practicing, some things will be confusing. Let me explain.

When I was younger, sixteen or so, I read everything I could find on sex. I hadn't had sex; because once you have had sex, there is little point in reading – but before you have sex there seems to be a lot of point in reading, thinking, conceptualizing, looking at pictures … But once one has sex one realizes that all this conceptualizing can never touch on the beauty and the tenderness and the joy of it. The words about it certainly touch something in you, and provoke a reaction, but the real thing and the words turn out to be very far apart. So it is with Dharma. You read and consider and think and practice and have small tastes that dissipate like mist. It is natural to form conclusions all along the way but it is useful to understand that those conclusions will always be mixed with confusion and delusion and, at best, be only partially correct. Sadly, all along the path, people form dogmas from partial understandings and then cling to these "lesser gods." This is why Rumi wrote, "I am the slave to that one who does not mistake every rest stop along the path as a final destination."

You ask, "How does compassion, which seems to arise between two entities, have a place in the non-dual state where there is no duality, no two entities?" This confusion is natural when one is thinking about non-duality – thinking about something that cannot be captured in thought. In the natural state compassion is the natural responsiveness of awareness. It is like the sun shining on many differing plants. The sun does not "think" it should shine, shining is just its nature. In the same way it is simply the nature of awareness to spontaneously respond exactly as needed in each circumstance without any notion of someone responding.

I call it the nothingness state because there are no "things" in it. Mind abides in the vast of Dharmakaya, and shines outward as joy and beauty, and encounters appearance as its own playfulness – encounters with love only. Love is the wish for others to know one's happiness. This naturally elaborates as compassion, which is the activity of removing others' suffering. This freedom is joy and love, radiant to infinity, through-as-in-of everything and every thing. To be nothing is only joy, to abide in nothingness, to have no formed structure or identity, let alone the idiocy of status or authority. From this empty purity only compassion and love, playfulness and beauty shine forth, and infinity extends as that. The sage encounters the suffering of beings as merely a blockage in the flow of love, and then the force of love works to undo that blockage. Whether they appear kind or wrathful, whether they use outer, inner or secret means, their method is just love acting to remove the stuckness of suffering. Mind abides not "in" but "as" nothingness (no-thingness) and from that radiance flows out and compassion is enacted spontaneously.

From the nothingness state awareness pervades appearance, the way wetness pervades water, sweetness pervades sugar, or warmth pervades flame; it is the emblem of mind's

. Love is the emblem of wisdom and compassion
ity of love. For one whose mind is immersed in
freedom, compassion arises unhindered from the ground of
phenomena's unborn nature. Have you ever thought about
the way clouds are the result of sunlight? When the sunlight
meets the earth, it warms the earth, and water evaporates
and rises into the sky to condense and become the spring-
time rains. When one whose mind is immersed in freedom
encounters a being in suffering, the natural warmth of
compassion coalesces in union with the person's suffering. It
coalesces into the responsive richness of love. A Dzogchenpa
can manifest in any appearance, but they always have the
same essence, nature, the same energy – and this essence
is primordial purity; and nature is radiance, spontaneous
display; and the energy is unceasing, heart-rending love and
compassion.

For a Dzogchenpa, one rested in the natural state, whose
practice is the display of the natural state, all behavior manifests spontaneously as what we call third conduct. First
conduct is the conduct in accord with the path of monks
and nuns, the conduct of renunciation. Second conduct is
Mahayana's conduct of compassion, and third conduct is
Vajrayana Tantra's conduct in accord with fearless spontaneous activity. This activity is not problematic so long as
mind is authentically rested in the natural state and conduct
arises as the ten virtuous activities – the display of the qualities of wisdom. For a Dzogchenpa, even if confusion arises it
is liberated on the spot. One hears this bantered about a lot
in Dzogchen circles but …what spot? That is the question no
one seems to ask even though by and large they don't know
the answer. What spot? There is an actual spot, a point, in the
way appearing arises from emptiness that is in fact "the spot."

The spot: The point, the place, the moment when the
luminous nature of clarity might by chance confuse itself as

somehow different, separate from the ground of phenomena's empty purity. That is the spot where dualistic consideration arises – the moment the luminous clarity surges forth from the empty spaciousness of purity (and this is every moment). In that moment the cognizant aspect can confuse itself as a subjective entity witnessing the luminous shattering of light as a playful frolic in empty space. It confuses itself as a separate subjective knower, and appearances as externally existent objects. Then, apprehender and apprehended arise, subject/object, self/other. Then, mind is confused about itself, by itself, it wanders in the narrow constricted pathways of endarkened unenlightenment.

Why is mind confused about that? It is confused about itself, about its actual essence of empty purity and its own nature of luminous clarity; it is confused about how empty purity and luminous clarity within union give rise to magical empty appearances. So what is it confused about, about Itself! And how has it come about this confusion? It comes about this through Itself as well. It is confused by its own playful frolic. This is always surging forth in luminous display, an unceasing manifestation as temporary modifications of luminous wonder, because of this there is the potential for confusion about objects. So it is confused about Itself and the confusion is caused by Itself.

Now I am not implying any sort of "Self" as an existent in this "Itself," it is only a figure of speech. As Wittgenstein said, language falls apart without the verb "to be," and here we are talking about things that do not include the verb "to be." So "Itself" does not imply a self of any sort. A self-cleaning oven does not have a little self inside of it that cleans. There is no tiny little man somewhere inside the oven, or some volitional, intentional consciousness.

So I am coming back, in just a second, to compassion in the natural state, the nothingness state, the wisdom state.

In such a state, which is no state at all, but beyond all states, appearances not only do not seem to imply duality they actually definitively prove to mind the luminous playful wonder of non-duality. Even as appearances arise, wisdom's own force causes mind to inhere within the unfractured womb of wholeness. And, if this happens, then fear and desire can have no foothold. Where fear and desire have no foothold there is infinite radiance of the unsullied purity of mind – and that radiance is known by mind itself as love. It is felt as by mind itself as tremendous tender heartedness. Then appearance, in and of itself, is playful beauty only. When awareness encounters the constriction of delusion and suffering, suddenly, without ever changing in any fundamental way, it becomes the activity of compassion. Because the inherent radiance of wisdom awareness is luminosity, is utter joy, perception is pure pleasure. Joy naturally generates love that is the wish for all beings to know this happiness. Love naturally becomes the activity of compassion, the removing of the causes of suffering. If a dualistic, confused, suffering being is encountered, then the magical alchemy of awareness that can turn itself into anything needed – does so. Without ever leaving the equanimity of the womb of suchness.

This is how four immeasurables – joy, love, compassion, and equanimity are the natural stage of Dzogchen. The word for the energy of awareness, in Tibetan, also has the meaning *perfect responsiveness* or *compassion*. Awareness is perfectly responsive, and so, when it encounters suffering, it experiences the heartbreak of compassion in a way non-dual from the object of compassion. It is because there is no alienation between the compassion and the suffering, the sage experiences what Jesus meant when he said, "Love your neighbor as yourself." He meant as your Self – literally. This non-dual compassion, this tenderness, gives rise to spontaneous responsiveness, the wisdom cure for suffering.

So a Dzogchenpa may appear in the most ordinary fashion, or in an outlandish fashion, or both, or something else entirely – there can be no limit or restriction … but they are never ordinary in the sense of manifesting deluded conceptuality because all conceptuality is released, liberated, in the moment arising on the spot where confusion could take place. Mind is always held in the nothingness state where luminous radiant non-duality, which is joy, love and compassion inseparable from equanimity, shine forth. So, there is no problem, in terms of compassion, for one who actually is immersed in freedom. Their compassion never wanes and never ceases. It is like the moon that is actually always full – all month long. The moon only changes, waxes and wanes, according to the partial dualistic view of sentient beings on earth. But the moon from its own perspective is always full. The sun from its own perspective is always shining and bright. But from partial view on earth, it seems sometimes covered by clouds, seems sometimes to disappear in night, sometimes to arise in dawn, but from the sun's view, perfect completion is always shining, always bright, always the infinite brilliance of love and compassion. When you come to the fullness of experience through sincere, earnest practice of Vajrayana's sublime methods, you will understand more fully. Until then, may my words act as a pointer and may all beings know an end to suffering.

With sincere best wishes,
  This vagabond yogi

Dear Friend,

You ask about joy and its source and it seems that perhaps you think that joy arises from particular externals involving time, place, or the people you are with. But I suggest to you that these are at best shallow and temporary sources and always tinged by anxiety. Why tinged by anxiety? Because all circumstance, substance, and relationship is impermanent, and so even if we are fortunate enough to have momentary pleasant circumstances we know it cannot last and hence there is anxiety. Perhaps you think it is depressing to consider in this way, but no more depressing than suggesting to an alcoholic that alcohol is an unreliable friend. If there were no other option it would be depressing, but perhaps fixation on externals is blinding you to some greater possibility. This is the advice of all sages, Buddha, Jesus, Krishna and myself – come and look, come discover the hidden possibility. It is only hidden as a result of not looking.

What if the longing within your mind, heart and body was whispering to you of truth? What if your deepest nature was not sin or confusion and did not end in death? What if Original Innocence, untouched by birth, death, comings or goings, untouched by impermanence, anxiety, fear, hope ... was, in fact, your true nature? True of you. Just waiting for an invitation to reveal itself?

Feel it for a moment. Original Innocence. Just say the words out loud and feel them. What if the heart of your heart was not marked by any stain. Not the stain of original sin, not the stains of mistakes made, not the stain of death or love lost? What if the wave was not isolated, alienated and alone against the world of other waves? What if the wave was in fact nothing but the ocean's temporary play? Feel it. Breathe it deep.

People become scared to hope, this may be true. Their confused searching over such a long time (lifetimes) has lead to endless small pains and great heart aches, and one decides, "I can not trust again. I can not trust this longing in my breastbone, this ache for freedom in my head." This sort of jaded nihilism is the greatest sadness possible. Still, no matter how jaded, how depressed the body mind becomes, the possibility of freedom remains.

What must be understood is that the heart of wisdom is Original Innocence and Bright Virtue – this authentic reality of Buddha Nature has also, from the start, been the very basis of mind's natural state. Your own mind, as it is, is rooted in this natural state of Original Innocence. Mind becomes fixated on content. Our whole philosophical tradition is deeply grounded in Descartes' "I think therefore I am." And yet there are moments in each day where we do not think at all. What then? Mind's activity is the content of mind's vast essence of Original Innocence and nature of Bright Virtue. These two are the very context in which the content takes place. They are not like a container and what is contained. Mind's essence and nature are more mysterious than that. What they are cannot even be known, and yet one can sink down into them and participate in their mystery. If you do this, body and mind's activity and feeling become accustomed to ease that is otherwise not known, a joy without the seeds of falling back.

This basis of mind's deepest reality is a mystery beyond all notions, all concepts – birth, death, being, non-being, color, attribute, shape or size. It is an expanse of sublime spiritual mystery. When you come to recognize your own mind's deepest reality you will have come to know the Original Innocence and Bright Virtue of the divine. Even more profound and amazing is that when this deeper reality of mind is known, the truth of all appearances is also known – the manner in which all appearances are held in-as-of this very expanse. Everywhere and every appearance is always only and forever nothing other than the ornament of primordial purity and luminous spontaneity.

Confusion, the deluded state of confused identity, is like a mirror that mistakes itself for the content of reflections upon its surface. These reflections are constantly changing, and so the confused mirror would develop a deep, abiding and entirely understandable anxiety. The ever-shifting images in the mirror are like the content of mind, and the mirror's natural reflectivity is the context of mind. The mirror, like your mind, is empty of any image of its own. It is an open receptivity. The mirror's emptiness allows anything and everything to be reflected within it – without any judgment. That the mirror lacks any image of its own is its emptiness quality, its essence. The mirror's nature is its capacity to reflect, its open dynamic space in which anything and everything is reflected. The mirror's emptiness plus its reflectivity together create the images within the mirror. The reflections in the mirror do not disturb the mirror. They leave no trace or stain. They ceaselessly come and go and do not alter the essence or nature of the mirror. In the same way, experiences and actions, even births and deaths, come and go in the mirror of mind's essence and nature and no stain is left. No matter how many clouds appear in the sky, the blue sky always remains unstained.

The difference between a mirror and the mind is that the mirror does not hold divine secrets within it essence and nature and the mind does. The mind's nature is also reflective and it most astoundingly produces its own images from its luminous aspect. Within this expanse and luminous nature the images flow and change, forming temporary patterns. If the knowingness aspect of mind does not become confused by this process, then there is no problem and no suffering.

If the knowingness aspect does become confused, then it becomes lost in the unceasing labyrinth of infinite possible reflections. If this happens then panic sets in and anxiety twines its way into every facet of experience. Mind's confusion produces an identity, within a body, within a world, that has experiences.

In short, all appearances are not other than the spiritual potency of mind's great mystery, and mind itself has no basis. It is the function of the path to awaken you to this subtle wisdom understanding, but the wisdom itself is always true from the beginning. Wisdom, then, is to inhere in-and-as this truth without effort. The spiritual longing of every human being is to realize, make real in the continuum of life, body, speech, mind, this reality. To embody and enworld the beauty of Buddha Nature's expanse and luminous clarity is the meaning urge of our lives. The essence of spiritual reality, the essence of mind, is an expanse of unutterable mystery – perfect purity. The nature of this purity is luminosity whose radiance is a perfect clarity. These are the Original Innocence and Bright Virtue of your life waiting for you to discover and live them to the point of being translated into them.

Buddhas see only Buddha. Nothing other than Buddha Nature is seen by Buddhas. No original sin is seen, only some seeming beings mistaking their true nature for something more dim, less free. Buddhas do not see any actually existent suffering, no death, no birth, only the play of wisdom bliss, only Original Innocence. There is no expulsion from the Garden of Eden. There is only distorted vision unable to see the way things are in truth. The blessings of Buddhas and the path of Dharma are that which leads to clear seeing.

I am not saying these things as abstract philosophy; I am not saying them because they sound nice. I am describing direct experience. There is a path, a series of methods bring one to this realization. These methods have been tested in the laboratory of body and mind by women and men across centuries and continents. They are proven anew again and again. The methods make one's body, mind and feeling into subtle tools for spiritual knowing. The path is not easy, the path requires intelligence, courage, hard work, and independence … but, suffering is not easy either.

I hope this letter finds all of you well and happy and deeply engaged in the excellent path.

With aimless great affection,

t.

Dearest Friends,

So you might wonder how is it that if Buddha Nature is the only thing that is, how does delusion arise at all in the midst of this spacious luminous divinity? How does confusion even come into play if everything is light and wisdom as playful vastness? What is delusion? What is suffering?

When I was a young man, I spent a lot of time on the banks of the Kokosing river. I was supposed to be in class, but the water and the breeze through the trees called to me in some way. They offered an education that I found lacking in the college classroom. If you are truly alive, if you have a passion within you to know existence, to know it in all of its manifestation, its beauty and its ugliness, its pleasure and pain, life itself will teach you in every moment. The world is made up of symbolic presentations of truth. If your heart is open, the wind and the trees, the open fields and sky, will become your texts, your sutras. The great yogi Milarepa once said, "I am beggar with no books at all and because of that the whole world has become my library."

Sitting by this river over time, I learned a lot. In the beginning, I did not have much intimacy with the river and I remember thinking one day about how the banks shaped the river. But as I spent hours and hours floating in the water and sitting by the side of the river, enjoying the countryside there, I could understand that the relationship between a river and its banks is more organic and subtle. The banks and the river exist interdependently. Sometimes a storm, its swirling waters and changing currents, would carve entirely new channels, and it could be observed that the river was actually carving the banks and the banks were holding the river. Banks and water function in a way that blurs the edges of the boundaries in the pure process of appearing. One of the things I noticed, living by the river, was that sometimes, in a storm, a branch or a whole tree trunk would fall into the river, blocking the water's natural flow. Where the river was blocked, little swirling pools appeared. The trapped current would circle inside of a closed loop and that loop would become a small world of its own on the side of the flowing river. Sometimes, in the first day or so after they were created, the swirling pools would be really fun. You could swim in them, float in a little circle of swirling current – swirling vortexes created by the interruption of the river's natural flow. But after a few days, these pools would become repositories for all manner of trash and pollution. They would become foamy, stinking puddles of stagnation. They were still connected directly to the river. They were never truly separate from the river. But because the flow of the river was blocked, they formed a stagnant pool.

The nature of delusion is just like this stagnant pool – we have talked before about how the self-glow of awareness mistakes its knowingness and luminous aspects for subject and object. Well, when this happens the shaping of the subject/object duality becomes a pool of swirling light that collects the rubbish of confusion and delusion. It stagnates, resulting in notions of births and deaths and other painful-seeming separations which are mistaken assumptions made about the rise and fall of luminous waves of substanceless wisdom bliss. When the luminous knowingness of unborn wisdom bliss mistakes itself for a subjective entity, it clothes itself in a body, a world and a realm. These little pools are symbolic of the differing ways Beingness clothes itself as realm ... as human realms, animal realms, god realms, hell realms. Because there is infinite potentiality in luminous awareness it can form this into anything and everything – and it does! If wisdom is set free from confusion, the same space that once created problematic appearances is seen quite differently as simply playful divulgence of awareness' potency. Appearances become the playground where the rise and fall of Beingness displays the qualities of Buddhahood.

Now and then on the river, I would enjoy moving the log and stick jam and releasing the water trapped within. There would be a sudden influx of fresh water and suddenly all the flotsam and jetsam of stagnation would wash away. As you move through the path, this is what causes the ongoing experiences of bliss, devotion, wonder, joy. A practice removes a stick, a tree trunk, a collection of plastic bags blocking the flow of wisdom awareness and there is an in-rushing of joy. The function of the path is to remove the obstruction that blocks radiance to infinity.

The nature of awareness and its radiance wish to move ceaselessly to and through and past infinity as all possibility, and when they become blocked, they feel stagnant and seem to result in a sentient being. To be a being is to be a pocket of stagnation. What is in reality a pocket of perfect non-duality now becomes a seeming duality of subject and object, self and other in a world that feels insecure and full of dualities like pleasure and pain, loss and gain, fame and shame, praise and blame. The blockage is in perception. Pure perception of how things actually are becomes confused perception, stagnant perception. The TRUTH of how things are is quite divine; it is splendor only, unspeakable perfect freedom and silence, deathlessness and the mystery of godliness.

This is my invitation to you. This is the import of the Buddha's teachings. It says in the Avatamsaka Sutra that there will never be a place or a time anywhere, in any realm, where countless Bodhisattvas, fully enlightened Bodhisattvas, are not manifesting for the benefit of beings. This is because even the stagnant pool is never separate from the river. The pools of beings are not separate from the divine and so the divine can sparkle through and intervene in the affairs of ordinary beings. One who has realized this, who is not lost in delusion, is a force of intervention in the lives of apparent beings lost in suffering. Buddhas, the grace and beauty of authentic lineage and the Guru are all this intervention. I have come to know this truth and to live in this and as this truth; perhaps you are still seeking, but there is no real difference between us – both are the river's water. Original Innocence and Bright Virtue are my truth and they are also your truth. This is so because there is no separate you and me within that perfection.

If we understand how delusion arises from the first losing of this mystery beyond consciousness, prior to consciousness, prior to being, we can begin to understand the nature of the path, which returns us to this state of knowing. Within the path the methods are laid out with great detailed clarity. It is my hope that you will take this path to heart, chew on it, contemplate it, practice it, realize it and make it yours.

With love, t.

On the Guru Tradition in the West and also Ants, Spiders, Lions and Eagles

Dear Friend,

You write that perhaps you ask too many questions. Please do not worry in this way. One of the advantages of dharma's arrival in a new culture is that it requires those of us who understand the function and methods of dharma to apply our wisdom understanding to discriminating between what is meaningful to beings in a different culture and what aspects of the teachings are the result of unnecessary culturally based trappings. Over centuries of time, every tradition accumulates accretions of useless social trappings like barnacles on the side of a ship.

In your letter you ask, "Can we in the West, having no cultural parallel to the Vajra master, ever make use of this relationship in a sane way?" You quote Kipling's line "East is East, and West is West, and never the twain shall meet." I was reminded of having heard this not long ago. A few years ago I was at a conference on Buddhism in America where a discussion was taking place regarding the difficulty with acceptance of the "Guru" or "Vajra master" in Buddhism's transition to the West. People talked of how, because there was no parallel institution or concept in the West, there was no ground for true understanding of this relationship. It was suggested that perhaps other models, more up to date and culturally pertinent, could be useful. It was suggested that perhaps a "collective wisdom of the sangha" could function as guru, or perhaps teachings from rotating teachers or some sort of co-counseling dharma format in which each person helps others by sharing insights could be substituted. At the end of the discussion one lady softly said, "East is East, and West is West, and never the twain shall meet." Everyone chuckled and went to lunch.

Your question is not unique and I can certainly understand how you find yourself wondering this. Like most of the people in that conference you would, I believe, think yourself liberal, open minded and multicultural in your view, as well as highly educated and intelligent. For this reason the question's bigoted, racist view in support of a narrow, white, protestant, anti-minority vision of Western culture and history surprises and saddens me. But because you also seem sincere in your search, I would like to take some care to explain this vital point.

The real question is not one of cultures, as precisely this relationship has existed in all Western cultures, within the domain of serious esoteric spiritual practice. A comparable role to that of the Vajra master exists in all three major Western religions in their esoteric aspects; we will discuss these in a moment. Even if it were an issue of differing cultures, would you advocate closing the borders of our minds against free trade? Are we so disturbed by the current multicultural state of affairs that we would like to form an Office of Homeland Security for the mind? The understanding of impermanence is the core of Shakyamuni's gift to us. The truth of impermanence is transcultural and applies even to cultural paradigms. The history of human development is the history of peoples intermingling, mixing and learning from one another. Are we so arrogant that while exporting our Coca Cola Monsanto sexualized marketing democracy we will not accept wisdom imported from other cultures and times?

It is worth noting here that Kipling's poem ends:

But there is neither East nor West,
Border, nor Breed, nor Birth,
When two strong men stand face to face,
tho' they come from the ends of the earth!

Before we look at how this question is based in lack of knowledge, in both its historical and cultural aspects, I would like to look at one more issue. When you say, and I suspect you simply parrot what you have heard from the purveyors of mediocrity, "Can we, as a culture, do this or that?" I am wondering what are the implications of this "we." Why do you say "we" and not "I"? Why not say, "Can I make use of this relationship?" If you ask in this way, the responsibility for making use of or not making use of the relationship falls squarely on you. The implication of this "We in the West ..." is that there is some sort of group-think which determines the actions of individuals. Is there some committee that will decide what religious style we will all follow "in the West"? Who are they and when were they given this power to make this decision for you, for me? When we say "we" in this sort of question "we" lose our dignity, our freedom, our individuality, integrity and responsibility. Precisely the things that many fear they will lose if they have a Guru!

If you take responsibility for your own actions you will feel great strength and joy. You do not need to be part of some imaginary "collective whole" which seems fashionable in superficial Buddhist circles. Perhaps some overarching bureaucratic superstructure Buddhist church will be developed in the West through centuries of Buddhism conferences. Its pews filled with the dharma flock will feel comfortable and safe within the herd pen of exoteric social dharma. But those individuals who wish to follow the sublime path of esoteric realization will be drawn to the ancient and modern, Eastern and Western, ways of authentic transmission from great realizers. The real issue within your question is not one of culture or Western history, but one of the distinction between exoteric social religion with its social conformism agenda and esoteric spiritual processes concerned with realization of Truth.

Within the spiritual longings of human beings there has always been a dynamic tension between the exoteric social and esoteric individual aspects. When we look at Western history and culture, as we will in a moment, we discover that the relationship of the student to the realizer, such as Vajra master, Guru or Lama, has always played a significant role in the esoteric traditions. The exoteric aspects of all religious traditions have always offered a consoling socialized religion in which the collective can be instructed in what is "right" and "wrong" so that society can function smoothly and people can feel connected like a nice flock of sheep. Yes, Buddhism is following this trend as well, and it is a good thing, as this meets the needs of the majority of people. The esoteric path, which is what we are talking of when we talk about Vajrayana, is a path of individual decision.

The esoteric path always comes with warnings: be careful, do not enter without great forethought and preparation. As Trungpa Rinpoche said, "Best not to begin at all." The esoteric path is for those who would storm the gates of heaven, whose hearts can only settle for firsthand experience. Only a small percentage of people feel compelled to look deeply for themselves into these matters and are willing to forge body and mind into the tools of such existential exploration. The real problem comes when people who do not really want to embrace the hard work, demands and profound individual integrity that the esoteric path requires, but they also do wish to buy or be handed the profound results. These individuals, who inevitably suffer from alternating childish dependency and/or adolescent independence issues, feel enraged that the "secrets" cannot merely be bought and sold for ego's profit, without the maturing demands of authentic, true and deep human relationship.

In the Tantric system it is often said, "This is not a path for *pashus*. Keep the secrets away from *pashus*." A *pashu* is a herd animal, a being who wishes to hide behind the safety of questions framed with words like, "Can *we* do this or that?" I am not trying to put pashus down; a pashu is a pashu, a tiger is a tiger. Ants have collective culture and spiders have solitary culture. Each type of being must find its own way. I believe in radical freedom, for the pashu's right to be a pashu and enjoy the collective pen. I believe that the lion should enjoy its pride and the solitary lone wolf should enjoy his solitude. But let us not pretend life is made of only one type so that we can impose the dictatorship of narrow conformist dogmas on "we in the West." The pashu does not enjoy the same freedom as the lone eagle, and the eagle would never wish it on the pashu. In the West there are many pashus, a few lions and an occasional lone wolf. Ants need ant dharma, collective and organized according to group mentality. Spiders enjoy spider dharma with radical individual responsibility.

So why do we need to decide what "we in the West" will have or can do? Why do we need to form "One Dharma"? I suspect it is because in every herd all are equal but some are more equal than others – as George Orwell presented in *Animal Farm*. In every herd, power mongers, disguised as pashus, wish for power mongering dharma – for the benefit of all. Mussolini originally wanted to rule the masses so that he could keep them safe and make the trains to run on time. Power monger dharma would like to impose collective dogmas on spider and ant dharma for the good of all and so that all can be harmonious under one dharma, their dharma. For this reason they do not feel a real need for facts or reason in their arguments if bigotry and deception will work instead … and so questions like, "Can we in the West with no cultural background in the Guru tradition yadda yadda yadda …." I can't say I care deeply what "the West" can do as I am more interested in what I, in my own personal responsibility and freedom, can do. But it is also simply incorrect that we do not have this tradition in the West.

> The Buddha said that the cubs of a lion enjoy their
>   mother's roar
> but to the pups of a jackal it is not so pleasant.

The exoteric has always had a certain distrust of the esoteric; the pashu has a natural ambivalence toward the tiger. The ant is not comfortable with the spider. The monastic bureaucrat is suspicious of the yogi, and the carefree yogi has no great desire to sit in Buddhist conferences. Many who enter authentic esoteric Vajrayana's lion style are happy to hear its roar. Others whose motives are impure, or who are more suited to the sheep's pen, or who become involved in Vajrayana in order to live out childish or adolescent complexes, find themselves very unhappy. Some, preying on the unhappiness experienced by those ill-suited to the path, would protect all types of people by forming safe enclosures. They would protect the river from the dangers of loving the ocean. They would protect the morning mist from the hazards of the warm sun's rays. They will stand up for the puddles right not to feel small in the face of the ocean's arrogant claims to vastness. They will protect us to death from the very birthright of our Buddha Nature and in exchange they will give us three meals a day in our safe pen and a good guard dog to keep us in! Then those of us whose hearts long for the heights, whose beings can never be happy in the sheep pen, will pace like the puma behind the bars of the zoo. I am reminded of a poem by e. e. cummings:

> When serpents bargain for the right to squirm
> And the sun strikes to gain a living wage –
> When thorns regard their roses with alarm
> And rainbows are insured against old age

When every thrush may sing in no new moon
If all screech-owls have not okayed its voice
– and any wave signs on a dotted line
or else an ocean is compelled to close

when the oak begs permission of the birch
to make an acorn – valleys accuse
their mountains of having altitude – and march
denounces april as a saboteur

then we'll believe in that incredible
unanimal mankind (and not until)

If it does not chafe at you to be lumped into a herd of
"We in the West," then may you live happily in the herd
enclosure of group think and may you find pure sublime
ant lineage to follow. If you wish instead to practice the esoteric path of Vajrayana then you can not coast on the decisions of group think and must consider each point with
care and honest individual introspection. If you decide to
leave the safety of the herd pen but your motives are impure or based in vanity, self aggrandizement, specialness,
then you will find yourself hurt by the external manifestations of your own deluded tendencies. Devotion for
the Tantrica is a natural love response to the divine lived
within the discipline and demanding rigors of absolute
self responsibility. Then you will not need the assurances
of herd shepherds as to democratic egalitarian fantasies.
For the Tantrica, acceptance of a higher power, a source
of blessing does not denigrate but enoble it, draws one
upward into an ever evolving wonderment of life. If your
heart and intentions are not pure it is your own falsity that
will lead you to a false Guru who takes advantage of your
self manifesting delusions.

Maybe the beauty of our Western traditions of Guru devotion will inspire you, for we have several. In all esoteric processes found in the three major Western religions, as in our own sublime Vajrayana tradition, it is not the techniques which take primacy but the relationship with the Vajra master. The Orthodox Christian Bishop Ware says so succinctly, "In the last resort, what the spiritual father gives to his disciple is not a code of written or oral regulations, not a set of techniques for meditation, but a personal relationship." Perhaps it is the fact that this relationship cannot be bought, sold, conquered or stolen that infuriates those who would reduce all spiritual life to consumerism in our mass-market quick fix cult of modern society. The demand of true, authentic relationship with the living presence of Truth is annoying to those who would retreat into isolationist caves of spiritual non-relationship like a dog who runs off under the table with its bone. Our culture is replete with the beautiful examples of this profound relationship. Let me explain to you.

The Vajra Master in Judaism

There are three major religions that shaped Western history. They are Judaism, Christianity and Islam. In Judaism, the relationship between the spiritual preceptor and the disciple finds its greatest blossoming in the Hasidic tradition of the Baal Shem Tov. This is an interesting example because it shows the emergence of a powerful Guru-disciple tradition in the midst of modern Western history! In seventeenth century Europe there was a revolution of joy within the Jewish community that has spread all over the world. This revelation and revolution was brought about by the power, realization and undying love of one man, the Baal Shem Tov, the Master of the Good Name.

The Hassidic tradition is a tradition of beauty, song and mystical contemplation. With the Hasidic movement came the flowering of the notion of the Tzaddik, the spiritual master. There is a Hasidic saying that goes, "Without the Tzaddik, even if there were a ladder to heaven, it would not work." The Tzaddik, the essential function of the "righteous man," has always existed in Judaism. As it is said, "The Talmud teaches us that G-D asks: 'Who rules over me?' and answers that it is the Tzaddik." (Sichos HaRan) But it is with the generations following the Baal Shem Tov that this took the true form of the Vajra master / disciple relationship as a primary means of attaining spiritual realization. The great Hasidic Master Rebbe Nachman said, "If a person is not bound to a true Tzaddik, all his devotion is nothing but twisting and turning and pretending to be something it is not, as if an ape were pretending to be a human being."

One of the most interesting points of the Baal Shem Tov's revolution, which applies to our discussion, is the way in which it spread to all segments of society. The Baal Shem and his successors, the Gurus of the Hasidic line, attracted the rich and the poor, the good and bad, aristocracy and peasants alike. The call of the spirit is not constrained by any boundary of nation, cast or class. It is not a contrived "democracy" for it sees that not all people are cut out for the intense disciplines of the mystic path. At the same time it makes no distinctions according to temporary samsaric class, race, or gender considerations. This was true of the Baal Shem Tov's open revolution of joy, and it was true of the ancient Tantricas of India. Amongst them were found kings, prostitutes, beggars, scholars, monks, alchemists and thieves, all practicing under the roof of a single tradition.

The Baal Shem Tov gave birth to a home grown, uniquely Western tradition of Guru-disciple relationship. Within it, the disciple recognizes the Tzaddik as a source of blessing; and through respect, faith and devotion that blessings shower upon the disciple; and that relationship, along with the methods of the path, brings the disciple to spiritual liberation. The beauty and joy of this path is often spoken of in the disciples' works. Let me share some with you. I love these writings because I know, from the depths of experience, that they are referring to my own precious Lama.

> Whoever considers himself an independent existent cannot be in more than one place at a time. When a discreet entity stands in one place, it cannot be elsewhere. Thus, if one is engaged in Divine service, he cannot gaze at the world around him. However, one who is nothing can be present everywhere. Therefore, the greater the degree to which a tzaddik is incorporated into Divine nothingness, the more he is able to see what is taking place in the world. It is not that he stands in a high place far above the world, rather the category of place does not apply to him at all.
> – Rebbe Nachman, *Likutey Moharan* 2:58

> The basis of everything is to be bound to the tzaddik of the generation completely and to accept everything he says as correct, whether it is a major or a minor thing. One must turn neither right nor left from what he says, but simply abandon his own ideas as if he knows nothing except what he receives from the tzaddik. So long as a person retains even a residue of his own independent way of thinking he has not attained fulfillment and is not truly bound to the tzaddik.
> – Rebbe Nachman, *Likutey Moharan*

Simply to look at the face of a tzaddik is a very great thing. How much more so when one is worthy of speaking to him, and even more than this, when one hears Torah from his lips. But simply seeing him is very good in itself.

Whoever is truly merged with this name, which is the glory and splendor and true delight of the whole world, whoever draws close to the tzaddik and is subsumed under his name, through this his eyes are opened and he can begin to examine himself and see where he stands. Then he can return to God and cleanse himself of all of his evil characteristics. He will be worthy of perceiving the greatness of the Creator and of looking at the whole world with clear vision, because his eyes and his mind are opened by the true tzaddik, who sends light to the whole world.

It is impossible to gain any true conception of what the tzaddik is in himself. He is totally beyond our grasp. It is only through seeing his followers that one can gain some understanding of his awesome greatness. When one sees that they are men who have achieved great things and who follow God's path in truth, then one can understand the greatness of the tzaddik himself.

Telling stories of the tzaddikim, contemplating the wondrous things that happen to them by Divine providence, is very great. Through this, you may purify the mind and pass into the world of thought. However to pass into the world of thought, you must be silent. Even if you were to utter a holy world, this would disturb your state of mind. For thought is extremely high, higher than speech. Even if you remain still and do not speak, there may be distractions that disturb your state of mind. To remedy this, you must

purify your consciousness. This is accomplished
through stories of the tzaddikim.
                    – Rebbe Nachman, *Likutey Moharan* 1:234

Everything has a purpose, and this purpose itself
serves another purpose which is even higher. The
most important thing of all is the ultimate goal to
which everything leads: the joy of the world that is
coming. This is the final goal of the entire creation.
However no one except the tzaddikim can in any
way conceive of this ultimate purpose. To the extent
that a Jew is rooted in the soul of the tzaddik he too
can attain some conception of this goal, depending
on how far he has succeeded in breaking his anger with love. If he succeeds he will come to a level
where he can use everything in this world as a means
to attain this goal.
                        –Rebbe Nachman, *Likutey Moharan*

In this beautiful tradition of love and transmission,
beauty, compassion, love and mystic insight have been
passed from one generation to the next. If one's heart longs
for this mystic revelation, it overcomes all fear and shuns
protection.

The Vajra Master in Christianity

Christianity, of course, was from its origin based in the
tradition of the Guru and disciple. While the exoteric
churches have always maintained outward institutions
wherein the relationship with an absentee Guru (Jesus)
plays the central role, there has also always been an inner
tradition. The writings of the desert fathers, such as St.
Anthony, and the profoundly powerful mystic mothers

such as St. Teresa of Avila, St. Clare, and Christian saints such as St. Francis and St. John of the Cross make clear that they practiced the path of obedience in relation to spiritual mentors. The monastic tradition, and its parallel tradition of lay hermits, has always upheld the esoteric tradition of Guru and disciple. These esoteric traditions have not been kept secret but are not well known by outsiders because the demands of such a life are more than most people would wish to bear, and most people have no interest in learning about them. This is true in authentic Tantric Vajrayana as well, even if it would not seem so when it is sold everywhere these days in the marketplace of materialistic grasping. Esoteric practitioners have always been the small minority, those who wish to dive into the human spirit's greatest depths and return with the jewels of love and compassion for all beings.

The value of such authentic realizers and practitioners has always been recognized by serious religious and spiritual beings in all cultures – including ours. This is why there has also always been a tradition of giving financial support to those on retreat and to monasteries. Even those who would not wish to devote their own lives to attaining spiritual wisdom sometimes see the value in supporting those who do. Beyond this, those who understand the spiritual process also know that such beings' efforts ripple across the expanse of human mind and world as blessing. All esoteric paths can pose risks to the delicate psyches of human beings. It is easy to increase one's confusion and ignorance rather than cut through them if we only rely upon the closed loop of our mind's capacity to understand subtle teachings. Then the necessity of guidance from one who has walked before, who is a living emblem of the possibility, is understood. This is why the great St. Anthony, the father of the esoteric Christian path said:

I know of monks who fell after much toil and lapsed into madness, because they trusted in their own work ... So far as possible, for every step that a monk takes, for every drop of water that he drinks in his cell, he should entrust the decision to the Old Men, to avoid making some mistake in what he does.

The function of the *Staretz* in the Orthodox Church is equivalent to the Guru and is a beautiful example of the Guru-disciple relationship. The process of transformation, transfiguration and translation is of such subtlety that submission to the care of one who has gone before is considered tremendously important. This tradition of spiritual life is as alive today as it has ever been. Bishop Kallistos Ware says of this relationship:

> This figure of the *Staretz,* so prominent in the first generations of Egyptian monasticism, has retained its full significance up to the present day in Orthodox Christendom. "There is one thing more important than all possible books and ideas," states a Russian layman of the 19th Century, the Slavophile Kireyevsky, "and that is the example of an Orthodox *Starets,* before whom you can lay each of your thoughts and from whom you can hear, not a more or less valuable private opinion, but the judgment of the Holy Fathers. God be praised, such *Startsi* have not yet disappeared." (shared by an Orthodox friend)

The structure of this relationship is an organic hierarchy of wisdom. The compassion arisen from realization flows downward to the disciple. The structure of the relationship is based in love not power. The disciple's devotion flows upward to the realized one as a natural organic response to love embodied. Is there room for abuse of this? Of course. Human history is the record of beauty made into ugliness by delusion – and that is why on such paths one is *always* asked to take great care. It is necessary to evaluate and to carefully choose one's Guru. If one wanted to become a great pianist one would wish to find a master of piano, a trusted authority, to whom one could submit oneself for instruction. Because a spiritual teacher's authority is being sought in matters of the human spirit, one must be especially careful and practice discriminative wisdom in relation to entering into such a relationship. In the Christian tradition one is to look for certain characteristics in the spiritual master. Bishop Kallistos Ware says, "Although the Staretz is not ordained or appointed for his task, it is certainly necessary that he should be *prepared.*" The Staretz becomes replete with qualities through the inward journey and it is these qualities that attract students. Perhaps the most famous Staretz of the church was St. Seraphim who said, "Acquire inward peace and a multitude of men around you will find their salvation." The qualities of the spiritual guide are listed as "Insight and discernment … the ability to love others and to make others' sufferings his own, to possess love and the power to transform the human environment."

To me, dear friend, what is amazing and beautiful is that this role, the Guru, is found amongst the most serious practitioners of every tradition with such similar understanding of its import. It says in the Buddhist Sutras that Bodhisattvas will be born in every place of the world. These examples from Western tradition make this so very clear. One should choose one's Vajra master with care and then enter the path by degrees, contemplating each stage, its commitments and demands, with great attention. Once one has entered the relationship, one chooses submission as a joy, which purifies the mind and heart of all that would separate it from the

Buddhahood. This submission is not based in blind faith or in a childish need to be taken care of. The choice to submit is an individual choice born of strength – not weakness. The entry into the esoteric process is always this way. Of this point Bishop Kallistos Ware says:

> Such stories are likely to make a somewhat ambivalent impression on the modern reader. They seem to reduce the disciple to an infantile or sub-human level, depriving him of all power of judgment and moral choice. With indignation we ask: "Is this the 'glorious liberty of the children of God'?" (Rom. 8:21.)

In our sublime Vajrayana path it is just the same. No one asks you, or anyone else, to take up this path. You must come to the Vajra master and ask sincerely. There is no force or twisting of arms. You will always be encouraged to expend great effort, establish time and deeds, and prepare before making such a request. No one is benefitted by rash decisions in the arena of human life's most intimate processes. In fact, all the great masters of Vajrayana, such as Trungpa Rinpoche, warn disciples time and again to enter the path with care and great forethought. You must be very sure of your own motives and those of your guide. If you enter seeking self-serving gain, as most do, the relationship will be one of frustration. It will cause you pain. Of this there can be no question since this motive causes pain wherever one goes. You should not enter the path without carefully looking to see if you can live in harmony with the teachings and style of the master. The full blossoming of the relationship takes time and care. Outside of the grasping hope and greed of ego there is no reason to hurry in such a way as to cast discriminative attentiveness to the wind.

A final point Bishop Ware makes is that the spiritual father does not want your enslavement.

> *Do not force men's free will.* The task of the spiritual father is not to destroy a man's freedom, but to assist him in seeing the truth for himself; not to suppress a man's personality, but to enable him to discover himself, to grow to full maturity and to become what he really is. If on occasion the spiritual father requires an implicit and seemingly "blind" obedience from his disciple, this is never done as an end in itself, nor with a view to enslaving him. The purpose of this kind of shock treatment is simply to deliver the disciple from his false and illusory "self," so that he may enter into true freedom.

The Vajra Master in Islam

The exoteric social form of Islam is, at best, profoundly uncomfortable with the idea of mystical transfiguration. At the same time, Islam has from its beginning had schools of mystical transmission. At the heart of these lineages is the disciple's relationship as lived with the Shaykh, Pir or Murshid. In the Sufi tradition the intoxication that banishes separation between one's mind and heart and the mysterious dimension of divine love is bridged through disciplined mystical practice under the guidance of a spiritual master. This relationship with the spiritual master is not only at the heart of the path but is also the heart of the practice. The practices rest on the living ground of this love. In the last two decades, translations of great Sufi poets such as Rumi and Hafiz have made the feeling dimension of the guru disciple relationship available in every bookstore across the nation. They have become part of the fabric of our culture.

I am a river
You are my sun.
You are the medicine
Of my broken heart.
                    – Rumi

In another place Rumi says, "whoever travels without a
guide needs two hundred years for a two day journey."

Again and again throughout his poetry Rumi sings of
the joy, pain, love, sorrow and transformation that arises in
the authentic relationship between a spiritual seeker and "the
guide." Again and again, as one who has walked the whole
path and is lost in the wisdom bliss of realization, he speaks
of the need for a guide and the dangers of not having one.
"Do not spurn a guide," he says. "The guide," the spiritual
master, is nothing short of divine intersession.

On the mystical path of Islam the student studies under the guidance of a master until both are deeply satisfied
regarding the sincerity and competence of the other. It is at
this time that the master chooses to initiate the student into
the order. Within the initiation, both accept the mutual bond
or pledge, what in Vajrayana we call *samaya*. The disciple
pledges to follow the spiritual guidance of the master implic-
itly. The master pledges to never forsake the disciple and to
guide them through the stages of the path.

The living transmission from heart mind to heart mind
must take place in a context of tremendous human maturity.
Problems arise when the master or disciple fails to cultivate
this context. The mystic path is not without trials. One must
trust that the master is always and only interested in the
disciple's advancement.

I said, "Thou art harsh."
He replied, "Know

That I am harsh for good, not from rancor and spite.
Whoever enters saying, "This I," I smite him on the brow;
For this is the shrine of Love, o fool! it is not a shelter
　　for sheep!
Rub thine eyes, and behold the image of the heart.

– Rumi

For the disciple, faith and devotion develop naturally
over time as the love response to what is sublime. For one
who is suited to the esoteric process, the relationship with
the authentic master is not one wherein we feel degraded or
belittled. It is the crucible wherein the gold within our being
is purified and revealed. The great sculptor Rodin said of his
work, "I do not create. I strip away and reveal the essence."
It is in the face of the beloved, the spiritual master, that
one comes to know one's highest potential, reflected not in
sycophantic imitation but in the true flowering of unsullied
wholeness in all its manifestations. When Rumi wrote of his
master Shams he said:

In my passion for His reality not even care of safety
　　remained.
By the grace of His help I become safe.*

Dear friend, I know this has been a long letter and I
hope there has been some benefit to you in it. It is my prayer
that you will not allow the purveyors of shallow consumerism to blind your eye to the beauty of differing styles and
approaches to wisdom. Let us all be happy to be sheep, ants,
spiders or tigers. Because we are also human beings engaged
in the spiritual pursuit we can learn to accept and even re-
joice in differences.

* from *The Wisdom of the East, Persia Mystics, Jalalu'd-din Rumi* by F.
Hadland Davis; originally published by John Murray, London, 1912.

Those who wish to enter the sublime esoteric Vajrayana path may do so only by accepting the relationship with the Guru. Guru is a fundamental axiom of Vajrayana. Those who do not want a guru can practice other Buddhist paths that do not depend on this relationship. Find a path you can love, a path whose tradition displays its power, grace and beauty and bind yourself to that path. Look and consider with care but then enter wholeheartedly as a warrior of compassion. This will give great meaning and joy to your life.

With love,
    T.

Dearest Little Birds –

Truth moves the sage's toes in glee. Reality enbrightens their fingers. You need to know this. Realization is not some abstract, it is not passive, it does not fail to transform body and mind. The Sage's whole being, body, mind, toes, arms, elbows, knees, bone, flesh, marrow become bright with this knowing.

Reality is announced by infinite silence. Truth is proclaimed in the absence of all conceptions, a stillness of mind so deep that even the urge of Being is laid to rest and there pervades only expanse, luminous and silent. Buddha Nature is then known in body as perfect freedom and joy. Joy, a force, a wildness, a happy proclamation – not in words but in tender movement of radiant brilliance unobstructed by any and all or no one and none. When mind is freed from its conceit then beauty, play-full-ness, creativity shine as joy in, into, through, beyond, embracing, untouched, perfectly pervasive of every thing, everything, and then some.

The one who realizes this is not bound, is not free, is not in delusion, is not in liberation, is not this or that, here or there. The one who realizes this is not silent or loud, they are not well mannered or crazy. The one who realizes this is free as emptiness, free as appearance. Do not expect them to forever pretend to agree with your small, contrived worlds of narrow strictures. Do not expect them to smash your conceits. Do not expect them to behave themselves according to your dictatorship of ego. Do not expect them to be storm troopers of glorious liberation. They simply are what they are beyond is and is not.

With love, t.

Dear Blind Donkey,

We must learn from everyone, swordsman, carpenter, baker, tree, wind, sky, child's car seat, mushroom and eggplant, ankle, thigh, hawk ripping out guts of mouse, black night, early dawn and midday in between. Mind must stop NOWHERE.

What do I mean by mind must stop nowhere? Awareness is radiance to infinity from a mystery without center or circumference. Its only urge is to shine to infinity touching along the way all appearances, the play of its own luminosity. It touches gently without stopping, it shines in-as-of-through each appearance. When it does this, things remain free. When it stops to form opinions, judgments or concepts about appearances it is required to dim itself down in a recursive loop. This loop creates the "self" with its identifications and confusions. Left unhindered, awareness is filled with simple Gnostic transconceptual knowing.

Let me use the words of the great Takuan to further explain. Takuan Soho was Zen Master and friend to the great swordsman Mushashi. In a letter he wrote to Mushashi's rival, he elucidates the mind that never stops and is also called "immovable." (Only the immovable can be called "never stops" and only that which never stops can be called "immovable.")

Takuan:

> ... and the mind which never stops is called immovable. Fudo Myoo grasps a sword in his right hand and holds a rope in his left. He bares his teeth and his eyes flash with anger. His form stands firmly... he is immovable wisdom.
>
> Seeing his form, the ordinary man becomes afraid and has no thoughts of becoming an enemy. The man

who is close to enlightenment understands that this manifests immovable wisdom. What is called Fudo Myoo is said to be one's unmoving mind and unvacillating body.

Glancing at something and not stopping, the mind is called immovable. This is because when mind stops at something, as the breast is filled with various judgments, there are various movements within it. When its movements cease the stopping mind moves but it does not move at all.

If ten men, each with a sword, come at you with swords slashing, if you parry each sword without stopping the mind at each action, and go from one to the next, you will not be lacking in a proper action for every one of ten. Although the mind acts ten times with ten men it never halts even once, never stops.

– *The Unfettered Mind*

This is beauty, this instruction is wisdom for going beyond the narrow box canyon of birth and death. Dearest friend, learn to allow the mind to move to infinity at which moment it is immovable – it is the protector of dharmas, Fudo Myoo (Achala). When the mind stops at "objects" and "things" then the sword has already cut you down – no enemy is needed; the sword of your own delusion slashes the vein of life. Mind is merely radiance of awareness. Radiance wishes, longs, is determined to move beyond all "things" and shine through all appearances (revealing them to be empty appearance and appearance emptiness) until it reaches the limitless limit of infinity. When mind stops nowhere but shines infinitely then it is immovable and it is also Love. This is the only true love. This is the love that raises the dead slain on the battlefield of never having truly lived. May it raise your own zombie corpse and bring you beyond the boundary of birth and death.

Let us learn from swordsmen both how to live and how to die and how to go beyond both.

Let us allow our love to outshine all stopping until moving reaches the immovable.

With love,
This scabbard of the sword of Love.

Dear Friend of our mutual Friend,

In response to your sad letter. Why? Why live in narrow boxes called "life"? Why make your home in a prison? Why settle down and become comfortable in the ramshackle rooms of samsara? This human life is, in and of itself, quite confusing and painful. Some traditions teach that you were meant to live well in this life in order to achieve a better life after death. What a sad notion. But this life is not "for" itself either. You are meant to live this life as ornament, as display of that greater life that is always already present. You are meant to be rooted in the Dharmakaya, radiant in the Sambhogakaya, and to live expression of that in this place. Anything else leads to suffering. So, this life is an invitation – not a tomb, not a graveyard as you suggest.

Appearances are seduction – seduction into wisdom or seduction into bondage. If you don't find their source, their origin, their ground, their substance within their substance, then your life WILL be bound by triviality and you will die without having lived. Exactly as you feel is happening. But that is NOT the only choice. All these so-called needs, wants and demands are the planks of your coffin. Your comfort, your routines and your consolations are the nails. But there is another choice … life itself is inviting you out beyond and beyond.

I am not saying you have to change external circumstances particularly. Your bondage is not caused by your spouse or children, job or home. The bondage of delusion is unrelated to external causes. It is created by mind, and mind accompanies you no matter where you go or what you do. Bondage is to live without diving into the mystery of what is and finding the depth and height of it. Some dive into the mystery through meditation born of pure sublime curiosity, some dive in through love – like a bee dives into the lotus blossom. Either way is perfect.

As we grow older we become more complacent. We become "at ease" with the way things are and decide that it is okay to conclude that our limited and unsatisfying life is all there is. A certain jaded cynicism sets in. This is especially true of the children of the '60s, like you, whose initial search was laced with so much confusion, self-centeredness and fantasy. They sought and searched and did not discover wisdom and then decided the teachings are a sham. Don't go with the flow – because unless you live as the ocean of realization the flow is only going toward death!!! As we grow old our bodies increasingly seek comfort. As we grow old our minds become complacent and weary. As we grow old, our heart settles for the status quo. We become swaddled in habits, we become sure of our actions, we become easeful in the day- to-day living of our life unto death. There is when it is most important to take up the way again! Having so much experience of the falsity of a life lived without having discovered a depth of meaning, we have so little left to lose!

Perhaps you think you have already taken up the way. But you must push further. You must confront the complacency of your mind and body and heart. You must look honestly at what caused failure before – look within yourself at your previous motivations and intentions. Ruthless self-honesty is needed. Over time we become convinced we have made real efforts. We look back on the retreats we have done, the mantras accumulated, the moments of insight and we sit back on the sofa of our contentment as death opens its gaping maw to swallow us whole.

I assure you, there is a way to truth. And if you seek this way both inside and outside yourself, and follow it with care, you will learn what the aging body actually wants – every day to rest the mind in bliss, the heart in silence, the body in joy – even if only for a moment. This is far better than the Tahitian vacation that has left you so depressed. Learn this and then let the logic of that love, that mystery, influence your actions. When you rest in bliss, and your body is full of brilliant love for all appearances – and appearances no longer act as bondage but as ornament – and the energy of awareness arises as actions for the benefit of all ... then don't rest!!!!! DON'T REST! Even then ... enact, embody, enworld!

There is no end. There is no destination. There is no stopping place. "Birds have their nest and foxes have their dens but the son of man has no place to rest his head." (Jesus) There is no peak of love – only a mystery where each peak of love opens the view to a new adventure, a new mystery, a new peak of LOVE ......

With sincere love,
    this

Hello Dear Ones,

Sitting here in a hotel room in Vegas, having finished *sang* offerings, resting mind in the infinite and deep beauty and joy – I think of all of you with happy heart, silent mind.

That which is the infinite well of empty open purity has no partiality at all … it is not for or against, it is not loving or hating, it is simply present while being nothing – no thing – whatsoever. It is not added to if you realize it and not taken away from if you don't – but you live in freedom, or not, accordingly. The ground of Mind is natural purity. That which is the deep well of luminosity has no enmity but is only the welling up and pouring over of the love to be. It is aimless great affection for all of Being's manifestations, whether they are considered good or bad by those whose minds are bound up in partiality. So give up disputation and put your energies into practice so as to realize this impartial great affection.

That which is a mysterious appearing falls to the side of wisdom or ignorance and, accordingly, one wanders in corridors of love and hate, pleasures and pains, seeking release but again and again finding only bondage. Like the people partying in the hall across from me all night – but then fighting with each other all morning. Like moths to flames – mistaking the entrance causes of pleasure and causes of pain. Please do not be this way.

Love, your friend,
t

Dear K,

"A lover doesn't figure odds." – Rumi.

You ask what I think of so and so's path … I don't! I think of how I can live my own more fully and deeply. How can I incarnate love more fully? There is a mystery that is extensive and pervasive and its name is Love. This love is an unutterable mystery beyond even the concepts experience and experiencer. It is extensive because its radiance is what becomes the ten directions and three times. There is no place, no spot, internal, external or in between where it is not – that it is not. It is pervasive because it pervades every cell, every atom, every subatomic particle and all of the space that holds these particles. It pervades them not the way wetness pervades a wet sock but the way wetness pervades a drop of water.

When in the deep of meditation your HeartMind comes to know this, there will be an end to chaos within the mind, for in knowing this one thing you have known every "thing" in its truth, in its intimacy. When in the depths of devotion, the body's natural love response to what is most sublime, this love comes to inhabit your doing and becoming, then the ten virtuous actions will be spontaneously manifest. It is natural pleasure, of the body's cells, of the mind's thinking, of feeling's longing, to stretch out into this mysterious wonder. The path is the how-to manual of this natural unfoldment. The path is walked as naturally as a snake uncoiling itself and moving forward.

The path is not an invitation to self-righteous superiority. Once entered into, our lives are lived in the Temple of Ruin. Love has broken down the walls of our desolation and isolation and left us under the open sky, revealed by the collapse of our guarded fears. This is the inner gift of taking refuge and Bodhisattva vows. Those who love the divine feel joy, joy grows into love, love into compassion and all is balanced in the discipline of equanimity.

Those who have entered the way will ceaselessly strive to love and enact, embody and enworld, love and friendliness. They will also ceaselessly encounter their own limitations on love and move beyond these limitations in the discipline of relatedness. This life, our loves, our families, our friends, our world is the ascetic's cave. Here, is the true renunciation where we turn our backs on the habits of unlove and rework our body, emotions and minds according to the beauty and demands of loving. Like gold, fired in a furnace to remove impurities, our lives are fired in the furnace of spiritual practice and the dross is burnt off. Like gold fashioned into countless ornaments – our lives are hammered and molded by love into the display of joy. There is no way to know what that display will look like. There are no dogmas or rules that can make safe the journey or dictate the outcome. Each being is too mysterious for that smallness.

The rose is not the majestic pine. Einstein is not Pablo Neruda. Buddha was not Krishna. I am not you and no other being will ever be you again. Each person finds their way in the world following the paths of their own choosing – the wisdom of those paths displays itself in the flowering of love or the frustrations of delusion. A path is a direction, not a dogma. The way is a yearning not a destination.

You have asked my opinion on so and so's actions – I have none. Why would I? I have an opinion on my own actions … I would like to learn to love more. How deeply and constantly can this body love, how deeply and fearlessly into life can this body's love go? My opinion is that that I should keep my attention on this matter rather than expend effort judging the spiritual path of someone I have never met. After almost fifty years of teaching philosophy, my father said, "What I have learned over time is that there are very few things I need to have an opinion about." I agree with him. You should follow your own intuition as to how you wish to live, but as you asked my thoughts, I have jotted down a few.

With love,
    t.

Dearest,

You recount your problems in meditation but I tell you that meditation is not about endlessly more new problems. If you follow this manner then you will turn the deity into a demon whose frustrations only insure ego's ever becoming stronger.

We come to spiritual life because we have known the taste of mystery and love. Perhaps we might think we come for other reasons. We might think it is to be "free," to overcome our problems, to learn to love ...... but the truth is that we are drawn by the intuition of a prior love, happiness and joy which can not be explained by anything in the world. This intuition has become a secret longing in our soul, in our heart, body, mind and moves us to discover its origin. It is the call of the Beloved. Yes the path makes demands of us to remove those obstacles to clear seeing, but it is always grounded in the prior intuition of a luminous expanse of unborn joy.

It is true that in our path we must "deal with" and overcome the manifestations of our suffering, but this is not because our suffering, mistakes, flaws, failure are somehow ultimately "True" of us, nor are they the proper objects of our meditation, contemplation, consideration. What do we as Tantricas mediate on? On wisdom's self revelation as felt images and imaged feelings of great sensual beauty – Tantric deities. Why? Because these forms of light and sound are deeply true of our own depths. They introduce us to ourselves.

So when you sit, when you meditate, do not make the problem of your life your focus. Instead, train mind in the disposition of love, devotion, beauty, wonder that are our practice. Meditate on love and mystery – and their union. When anything and everything arises – as it will! – don't fight with it. Instead recognize it as the play of mind's unborn luminous expanse – what in Tibetan is called *Rolpa Tsal*, the creative potency of awareness. Yes, you must discipline mind, because it has become fixated on some bad habits, but please, please do not turn this discipline into another reason for self concentrated suffering. That is not the path toward liberation but simply more ego reinforcement.

You have encountered the path, you have become a child of a noble family, you have received the inheritance of wisdom bliss through transmission and know the taste of love in relation to Guru and lineage. Within the world of appearances there are always more reasons to be unhappy than happy, but once one has encountered the sublime path of wisdom the logic of the world no longer applies. Be surprised by the fact that just these words can spark the feeling. Then apply it in the joy of the disciplines.

With love,
T.

PART III
ENTERING THE WAY

If one says existence, it is the eternalist extreme.
If one says non-existence, it is the nihilist extreme.
Whoever is wise does not remain even in the middle.
– The Sutra of Odsung

*Today, tomorrow, another day our parents and friends
will die, our lovers will die, our lamas will die, our possessions will scatter and be enjoyed by others, our own
aggregates will fall apart. Today, this evening, tonight –
soon all I cling to will be lost.*

– Lama Yangtig, Longchenpa

Dissatisfaction I

"Once upon a time that wasn't any kind of time at all. In a
mysterious non-dimensionality of mysterious expanse, there
lived an All Good King. This King was magnificent, blazing Bright Virtue." In Part I of this book I spoke of Original
Innocence and Bright Virtue as the essence and nature of
awareness. The union of these gives birth to the ceaseless
magical appearing child called appearance.

When the All Good Mother whispers in the ear of
Luminous Blazing what is heard? A vectoral feeling tone, the
feeling of dissatisfaction; a grinding, gnawing dissatisfaction.
A total dissatisfaction whose intensity can not be consoled
by anything or any thing. If you do not feel this then you
may hear something you wish to interpret as spiritual, but
you have not heard the first whispers of liberation as of yet.
The All Good Mother whispers in our ear and her whisper
causes the great dissatisfaction that can not be quenched by
anything in samsara.

So, there is nothing but this essence and nature of
awareness and the energy of awareness that manifests
awareness' potency as appearances. This is all there is.
There is *only* Original Innocence and Bright Virtue. So why
does there need to be a path, why work hard, why struggle with dharma's demands? Because, while this is true,
sentient beings do not realize it; they do not experience

it as the uninterrupted continuum of their body, minds, feelings. How to understand this? Well let's look at some examples from ordinary life.

My father had a friend, Eddie, in WWII who was in the trenches when a shell blew his best friend to bits right next to him. The bits, acting as shrapnel, had to be removed from his body. He had a total mental collapse and retreated into the protective belief that he was Napoleon. This delusion was all encompassing and covered over every bit of his life for almost two years while the psychiatrists slowly brought him back. He was not Napoleon, he was always already Eddie, and yet he was perfectly alienated from his life, his family, the world, lost in a dream designed to shut out reality. He was like Luminous Blazing lost in the endarkening land of ignorance. Like all sentient beings.

Another example is an anorexic girl. When she looks at her body in a mirror she literally *sees* herself as fat. Literally. She sees much of the world as it is but she can not see herself clearly. She mistakes various activities as sources of happiness – starving herself, excessive exercising – when they are, in fact, like the moth flying toward the flame, sources of terrible suffering. She even mistakes some forms, sensations, perceptions of suffering as happiness. To understand how one thing about oneself can be true and yet one does not perceive it at all, and suffers as a result of this misperception, is not so difficult to understand.

The very first step of spiritual life is tremendous, terrible dissatisfaction with the status quo of suffering in conventional human experience. When the All Good Mother first whispers in the ear of Luminous Blazing, in your ear, she whispers the magic spell that makes mind abide in the realization of inherent suffering built into the structure of the human realm's appearance. The inherent structure built into the structure of all appearing rooted in dualistic confusions.

In the first part of this book I spoke a bit about how appearance arises from the essence and nature; the union of emptiness and clarity. Appearing is not the problem. If it was then nihilism would have to accepted because there is no possibility of an absence of appearing. There are and will always be appearances appearing. As Longchenpa said, "Appearances are the inheritance of the Buddhas." To understand this point of inherent suffering within the realm of human experience is vital to any further travel on the path, so let's take a moment to review.

The boat may remain in the water, but if the water enters the boat, it will bring great catastrophe. Likewise, a person may live in the world, which is surrounded by the seas, but if the world enters the man, his whole life will be miserable.

– Ramana Maharshi, *Padamalai*, 295

๛

In the realm of culture, the new totalitarianism manifests itself precisely in a harmonizing pluralism, where the most contradictory works and truths peacefully coexist in indifference.

– Marcuse, *One Dimensional Man*, 61

๛

born born everything is always born
thinking about it try not to

– Ikkyū, *Crow With No Mouth: 15th Century Zen Master.* Versions by Stephen Berg, 20.

๛

You now have this opportunity of human life, so difficult to find; not as an ordinary person, but one who has encountered the Dharma …While you have the chance, and all conditions conducive to Dharma have accrued, even if you do not accomplish others' benefit at least practice for your own sake.

– Jamgon Kongtrul, *Creation and Completion*, 29

๛

One Ground, Two Paths, Two Results

The One Ground is the union of emptiness and clarity, the essence and nature of awareness. Whenever the luminous pervasion surges forth from the essence (and this is every moment) the energy of this surging manifests as appearances. This surging forth never leaves the One Ground; there is nowhere to go, there is no other "place" than the appearances themselves. There are two aspects – the knowingness and the luminous play as appearing. At the moment when the surging of appearance (and this is every moment) happens, two things also happen. Remember the universe of awareness and the salt shaker? When appearances surge forth: 1. The awareness knows the appearances and, 2. It knows that it can know. Prior to this there is only awareness unaware of its capacity to know. It is simply utter mystery even to itself. So, now there is the action of knowingness, this is the brightness of knowing – the appearances that the luminous aspect create through the play of its light. This opens the doorway to two alternatives: The knowingness inherent in unborn/undying wisdom awareness recognizes its own knowingness as inseparable from the absolute mystery of reality *and* recognizes the playful frolic of appearance as also inseparable from the absolute unfractured mystery of reality, or it doesn't. If it does then no matter what appears, doesn't appear, it makes no difference at all, for the vast expanse is unchanged and unchangeable luminous empty wonder. Now, if it does not recognize this, then the knowingness is mistaken for a subjective knower and the appearances for objectively existent entities.

If it is mistaken, then the point instant when the surging of luminosity, from-in-as, takes place, the knowingness mistakes itself for a subjective entity and that entity is felt as the feeling of Being. The I Am. Infinite, blissful and profound …… and wrong. The sense of existence, Beingness, the I Am, is the root mistake and building bloc of all delusion. Buddha was exactingly clear on this matter, as were other great masters like Nisargadatta Maharaj. The insight of Buddhahood, enlightenment, is beyond the touch of is and existent/non-existent, is/is not, Being/non-Being. It is beyond the touch of any concept, word or structure of human experience.

What happens when the unborn undying inherent always already mystery of wisdom awareness mistakes itself for a subjective entity perceiving actually existent external entities? Well, there is an apprehender and apprehended. There is a knower and known, subject and object. The appearances need "somewhere" to appear and so realms of "being" come into existence. The knower needs to abide in one of these realms so as to experience within it, and so Being becomes this or that being. A dog being, a god being, a human being …… Now Beingness, which was a mistaken narrowing of infinite mystery into subjective knower, narrows itself still further into the shape and form of a particular being and that being's experience of birth, death and experiences. If the mistake does not happen in that first moment, then appearances still go spiraling out from mystery as its own presencing of luminous play and they are, in some paradoxical sense, perceived (without there being anything that could be called a perceiver, perceived or perceiving). In Tantric Buddhadharma the enlightened version is called "the six expanse of the All Good Father" and the unenlightened version is called "the six realms." In one, Luminous Blazing plays in always already freedom of appearing and experiencing, and in the other, beings in realms experience appearing, plus individual identity, along with the inevitable suffering inherent in living a mistaken view.

At one point, in order to get out of the institution where he felt he, Napoleon, certainly did not belong, my dad's friend pretended he was Eddie. This did not work, because all his activities and mannerisms spoke to his delusion even when his words pretended to speak to having understood. The root structure of his actions and even experience was the persistent delusion of being Napoleon. For sentient beings the root structure of this realm itself, the mechanics of time, space, birth, death, is simply a mistaken shrinking down of perfect Buddha Nature in experience mediated by sub-ject-object dichotomy. It is a shoe two sizes too small – much like the Grinch who stole Christmas' heart. Sure you can walk in them, but they are going to hurt. Sure you might be distracted from the pain now and then by some fascinating moment of experience, but the hurt is still progressing, the blisters getting worse. This is *not* a nihilistic view. The prob-lem is *not* I appearances spiraling out from mystery, but in the wrong happening between the two paths and two results.

The One Ground is the perfect mystery that is the union of empty expanse as essence and the luminous clarity as nature. The two paths are seeing As It Is in reality; appear-ance as the perfectly non-binding modifications of mystery's luminosity, or devolving into the subject-object dichotomy. If it is the second, then it is simply a fact that all aspects of any realms structure is tinged with delusion in such a way that even the best moments carry a seed of suffering. This is lucky because it pushes beings to wish for realization of the reality that is wisdom bliss without the seeds of falling back. One ground. Two paths. Two results. Change the path change the result.

> Here are the miracle signs you want: that
> you cry through the night and get up at dawn, asking,
> that in the absence of what you ask for your day gets dark,

your neck thin as a spindle, that what you give away
is all you own, that you sacrifice belongings,
sleep, health, your head, that you often
sit down in a fire like aloes wood, and often go out
to meet a blade like a battered helmet.

When these acts of helplessness become habitual
Those are the signs.

— Rumi, *The Essential Rumi*, 11

Dissatisfaction II

The All Good Mother whispers in our ear and her whisper causes the great dissatisfaction that can not be quenched by anything in samsara.

Human beings do not so much have problems as they are problems unto themselves. The problem of the human situation and situatedness is built into the fact and act of being human. Samsara, beingness in delusion – which human consciousness is – is a disease … a dis-ease. The less mature a human being is the more they believe that there is some sort of fix-it that can happen in the context of the realm. In other words they think samsara can be fixed. A new car, a new home, a new relationship, more self esteem, a better homeland security … something in the realm of objects and relations. There are two problems with this: 1. Impermanence, and all fixes in the realm of things and relations are impermanent, and so ever the fix carries the anxiety of loss of the fix; and 2. The shoe of Beingness itself, let alone the shoe of birth and death, is two sizes too small.

> The soul that is attached to anything however much good there may be in it, will not arrive at the liberty of divine union. For whether it be a strong wire rope or a slender and delicate thread that holds the bird, it matters not, if it really holds it fast; for, until the cord be broken the bird cannot fly.
> – St. John of the Cross

Pervasive dissatisfaction, this is not merely that adolescent dissatisfaction with "society" or "the man" – some fantasy of how you have been held back due to race, age, gender, size, religion. Though all that may be relatively true, it is irrelevant to this discussion; social inequities are quite real and should be handled, but if that is the origin and limit of your dissatisfaction, if you can imagine a utopian solution, then your dissatisfaction is as yet quite immature. It is also not a dissatisfaction of circumstance. If you had better job, a relationship with your twin flame, if you went dolphin swimming and had an ayuhuasca adventure, a heart orgasm, this that or any imaginable experience ... even if the experience was uninterrupted ... if you feel this could assuage, console your dissatisfaction then you are as yet spiritual immature. This dissatisfaction understands, at least at an intuitive level, that the mechanism of experience is somehow flawed. At a much deeper level it understands that the concept "experience" is itself flawed as it will always contain the subject-object duality of experiencer and experience – it is always concerned with that which decays and is impermanent, which is everything and every thing. This deep problem has always been understood, and that is why from the Upanishads to the existentialist philosophers, amongst those of deep consideration, you find the phrase, "Where there is an other there is fear."

> Behold now, Bhikkhus, I exhort you: All compounded things are subject to decay. Strive with diligence!
> – Buddha, *Mahaparinirvana Sutra*

A freedom that does not have the seeds of falling back into unfreedom, a happiness that does not have the seeds of falling back into unhappiness, a life abundant that does not have the seeds of falling back into death – this is the real meaning of all human longing. This freedom, bliss, happiness must always already have existed and not be created, for then it could be destroyed. It must not come from or abide in the realm of created things – though it may well turn out that created things abide in and of it. Within the construct of human life this is not possible. This does not mean it is not possible for the quantity of awareness that calls itself a human being, it simply means it is not possible for that very limited, narrow, constricted configuration of consciousness that identifies itself as "human being." If the wave had self conscious self identification with itself as wave, if it felt its identity was the wave and limited its perception to any aspect of the waveness, then it would be cut off from the vast extent of the ocean. If the tip of the iceberg had self identity as the tip then it would lose its reality as the whole. If the hair on one's arm thought it was its own self then it would cease to enjoy participation in the wholeness of body. The human being is the tiniest bit of a bit of a bit of the whole and with its self identity as "human being" fretfully looking to fix samsara, make it work, convince itself it is all okay, it aggressively shuts out the true possibility.

No matter how you structure your life in accord with the axioms and dynamics of the human realm, suffering will be inherent. This does not mean there is no beauty, no pleasure, no temporary love. It does however mean that each and every one of these carries the seeds of angst, anxiety, hope, fear, birth, death within them. Where there is the feeling of a subject, an existent identity with its birth, death, attraction, aversion and indifference, there is suffering. Pure and simple, no way around it. If you can not understand this truth then it simply means your consciousness has not matured to that point. Happily, suffering is a patient teacher, and when you are done with endless strategies to make it somehow work from some or another configuration of objects, relations, state of consciousness you will understand. When you are as Trungpa Rinpoche used to say "hopeless," then you can begin. Hopelessness is the ground. Samsara, life in the human realm constructed from delusion, is always tinged with suffering. It is a hopeless situation. Every single atom of samsara and cell of the body wants it to be otherwise but it is not. My father's friend could not make life as "Napoleon pretending to be Eddie" work. There was just no way. Life as Napoleon also could not work because he was not Napoleon, and fear, suffering, angst were all built into the strategic system of thinking himself to be Napoleon.

Buddha's first noble truth, this whole matter discussed here, is a fierce argument with the rationale of human life, which can be summed up by the idea of being made happy. To be made happy by any object, relation, circumstance is simply to enter the realm of angst because you can then be made unhappy. Only a happiness that is always already and not based in even the physics of the human realm can be permanent without the seeds of falling back. Until you know this, in a stable fashion 24/7/365 waking or sleeping as lived experience, then you are right to be profoundly dissatisfied.

Listen fortunate one.
Now that your spiritual connection has been forged,
Achieve your eternal goals.
Strive on the sole path of all the victorious ones' heirs:
Generate compassion and the mind of awakening.

> – Dudjom Rinpoche, *Wisdom Nectar*, 99

∽

It is not a question of where you go, or whether you join a group. It is a question of whether you have been correctly prepared to learn how to learn.

> – Idries Shah, *Learning How to Learn*, 19

∽

Many things are necessary for observing. The first is sincerity with oneself. This is very difficult …We try not to see ourselves because we fear we shall suffer remorse of conscience. There are many dirty dogs in us, and we do not want to see them.

> –C.S. Nott, *The Teachings of Gurdjieff*

∽

Do Not Relax

There is nothing relaxing at all about Buddha's teaching. Buddha did *not* want you to relax. Anything but.

These days there is a lot of talk of meditation for relaxation. Well, that is nice, and it is lovely for people to relax – they need to due to the inherent stress of samsara. But, if you meditate to relax it has nothing whatsoever to do with Buddha's teachings or the deep of the spiritual path. Frankly, you are better off going to the spa, or a baseball game, or having sex, or playing backgammon, seeing a movie. You will get more bang for your buck in almost any of these. If you understand the first noble truth then you will feel deep dissatisfaction and this dissatisfaction will not allow you to relax. Frankly, you don't need to. It is not stress that makes you unhealthy, it is meaningless stress. Many people who feel connected to a great cause will work tirelessly to accomplish it; day and night, lose sleep, eat poorly under stress, and yet they are radiant and, in a relative sense, happier than most. Why? Because it is not stress but meaninglessness that crushes the human being in spirit.

Buddha said he was like a man who is walking down the street and sees a house on fire. Inside the house he knows there is a family fast asleep. They are about to die in their sleep. Buddha begins to shout and bang on the door to wake them up. He does not want them to wake up to their condition and then chill out, relax, try to sooth themselves. He wants them to wake up and experience the dread, what Gurdjieff called "the terror of the situation." They wake up, they smell smoke, they feel the heat, they realize their house is on fire and their children are in immediate danger of dying a horrible death as are they. This is *not* a relaxing situation. They work to do whatever they can to escape.

The night Buddha left home and family to engage the spiritual quest he stood in the doorway of his wife's room looking at her and his new born baby asleep. He loved them deeply, profoundly. He was not able to abandon them because he did not care for them, but because he loved them so much, and he realized they would experience sickness, old age, death, alienation, and all the sufferings that all human beings experience. He felt deep in the intuition of his human maturity that there was another option. He could not be satisfied with any shallow consolation sold by society or experience – even those of a prince. Imagine how he must have felt knowing his wife and child would feel abandoned. Yes, he expected to return with the teachings that bring an end to suffering – if he was right, but in the meantime they would feel hurt, abandoned, angry, betrayed. Standing there he must have been anything but relaxed. True spiritual aspirants are able to take into themselves the great turmoils of the human existential condition, they become an alchemical cauldron which can cook the stresses, tensions, facts of human experience. The All Good Mother whispers in our ear and her whisper causes the great dissatisfaction that can not be quenched by anything in samsara.

Marcuse and the Buddha, the Great Refusal

How can the administered individuals – who have made
their mutilation into their own liberties and satisfactions
... liberate themselves from themselves as well as from
their masters? How is it even thinkable that the vicious
circle be broken?
  – Marcuse, *One Dimensional Man*, 250-251

So, if you have the intuition of what is talked about in Part
I – Original Innocence, Bright Virtue, the child Luminous
Blazing – and you are not so pretentious as to convince
yourself you have already understood, then you will be
burning with dissatisfaction. You will feel happy that there
was someone like the Buddha who had the courage to say it,
to say ... there is something fundamentally wrong with this
whole game, the structure of experience and Being in duality
with its birth, death, separations, sufferings and also with the
forms society, and oneself, have given to manage it. Bravo!
Now you can join the Great Refusal. Herbert Marcuse, a
philosopher wrote about the Great Refusal in his 1964 book
One Dimensional Man, a book whose insights into the oppressive mechanisms of consumerist culture are more to the
point than ever.

Belief in the reality of the separate subjectivity is the root
of the problem Buddha resolved but it is also where we must
work, for it is us. The All Good Mother whispers in our ear
and her whisper causes the great dissatisfaction that can not
be quenched by anything in samsara. The creation of a subjectivity which refuses to participate in its own oppression
is the starting point of the path. Samsara, life in delusion, is
a rigged game. It can not work in terms of an end to suffering – this is obvious to anyone who looks with real care,

and is why Freud said the best human beings can do is go from neurotic misery to normal unhappiness. In the realm of death and separation, in the realm of alternating gain and loss, praise and blame, pleasure and pain, hope and fear, birth and death, in the realm where one thing eats another to survive there is no living without anxiety, and living without anxiety is exactly what the deep of the human longs for.

Marcuse's efforts to a solution failed. In the end, bound by the facts of the realm whose structure he could not transcend, his hope and fear led to bitterness. His longing for freedom, and the lack of society achieving that freedom, led him to develop angry systems of double speak where he espoused "repressive tolerance," sanctioning maltreatment of those who disagree with one, an "ends justify the means" foundation for revolutionary and psychoanalytic inquisitions. Sadly this is common, the ideals of Communism turn into the disasters of Stalin, Pol Pot's Cambodian Killing Fields and the failed promises of autocrats and dictators of the right and left everywhere.

> Those who promise us paradise on earth never produced anything but a hell.
> –Karl Popper (quoted in, *In Passing: Condolences and Complaints on Death, Dying, and Related Disappointments*, 2005, by Jon Winokur, 144)

Buddha's Great Refusal was truly "radical," a word meaning "to go to the root." Buddha went to the root of the problem of suffering; and the root is not in society, in government, in your childhood, in alien conspiracies; and its solution is not in harmonic convergences, political revolutions, psychoanalysis, dolphin swimming, drug experiences, spiritual visions, religious dogmas, technical exercises or any experience at all … it is in understanding the very structure of perception and experience. If you embrace Buddha's first noble truth then you will separate yourself from the fad of consumerism – worldly or spiritual. You will sever your relationship with the game of spiritual materialism.

> Thus, self-deception always manifests itself in terms of trying to create or recreate a dream world, the nostalgia of the dream experience. And the opposite of self-deception is just working with the facts of life.
> – Chögyam Trungpa Rinpoche, *Cutting Through Spiritual Materialism*

Marcuse spoke very directly to the fashion in which rich materialist culture uses endless streams of commodities as a means of oppression, a means of numbing oneself and the culture to the realities of social, psychological and political life. Trungpa Rinpoche spoke very directly to the way in which spiritual materialism, taking refuge in any state or meditational, drug induced, manufactured by spiritual techniques, hyped up blisses, emotional reveries, serve to numb one from the true process of spiritual life and actually increase suffering and the frustrations of grasping to alternating experience. Spiritual materialism dominates in a consumerist culture. Marcuse spoke strongly about the unfreedoms of consumerist culture, about the overarching domination of the human psyche by manufactured needs and wants.

> You will receive everything you need when you stop asking for what you do not need.
> – Nisargadatta Maharaj

Marcuse predicted that increasingly corporate interests, spoon-fed through ever increasingly subtle forms of advertising, would undermine authentic questioning and even the ability to rebel, much like the drugged citizens consuming soma in Huxley's social critique novel *Brave New World*. A similar scenario is seen in the Twinkie mentality of internet spirituality. Ceaseless cutesy affirmations of and assurances are aggressively spoon-fed an eager audience. We are assured that Buddha didn't mean that human experience was actually flawed, that *all of it* was tinged by suffering; we are comforted that there is a cure and fix to make *samsara* work; or the Tantras are quoted in Twinkie fashion, "*samsara* is *nirvana*," but without any real understanding of what this means.

I am reminded of a story. One day Buddha was teaching on Truth and a man, in the back, sat quietly listening carefully. The next day as Buddha walked with Ananda they passed a village where the same man was expounding the very words of the Buddha. Suddenly the Buddha spoke loudly saying, "Liar, liar!"

The man was shocked and replied, "I am only saying exactly what you taught yesterday."

The Buddha said, "Yes, and when I said it it came from my experience and was made truth by that experience, but as you have no such experience your intentions are quite different; you are a liar."

All this Twinkie spirituality with its endless reassurances, affirmations, smiley faces and hearts is nothing other than the advertising of samsara. Those who offer it up mean well in their confusions and delusions, but only serve the purposes of unfreedom. Pseudo Dzogchen and Advaitic teachings that emphasize that everything is already Buddha or perfect misrepresent the teachings of Original Innocence and Bright Virtue to bolster the unfreedom of complacency. Buddha's teaching is not meant to make you comfortable. Buddha's teaching is not meant to make you relax. There is nothing so disturbing to the construct of delusion as the first noble truth, and that is why pretty much everyone works to reframe it as something other than what it is. There is nothing marketable about it. In the *Padhana Sutra* Buddha speaks to Mara, the god of delusion:

> That army of yours, that the world with its devas
> can't overcome,
> I will smash it with discernment
> I will go about, from kingdom to kingdom, training
> many disciples.
> They – heedful, resolute, practicing my teachings –
> despite your wishes, will go where, having gone,
> there's no grief.

Be dissatisfied. This world warrants it. Even be depressed. This realm is depressing. Happily, when one has seen the terror of the situation, when one has felt the hopelessness of all strategies within samsara, the first two noble truths – 1. There is suffering. 2. There is a cause of suffering – are followed by the third, there is an end to suffering, and fourth, there is a path to that end. If there was only the mechanicalness of delusion churning through-in-as appearance, if it were 100 percent, that would justify nihilism, but happily there is something else. The whisper of the All Good Mother does not invite us to some variation on human life but to a radical alternative. When Buddha was asked if he was a man he categorically said "No." When he was asked if he was a god or demon he replied "No." When asked what he was he said "Awake." The alternative of true spiritual life is not a human alternative. The human alternative is contained within that which is reality, but reality is not contained within the human alternative. You are *not* asked to be something other than human in your body, mind, feelings, this content of your consciousness, but you are required to discover something far beyond "human" as the context of these.

Today, tomorrow, another day our parents and friends will die, our lovers will die, our lamas will die, our possessions will scatter and be enjoyed by others, our own aggregates will fall apart. Today, this evening, tonight – soon all I cling to will be lost.

– Lama Yangtig, Longchenpa

Without Origin

For there to be an "origin" there would have to be a "thing" which has origin and, as there is not, time dissolves in the equality of luminosity.

For there to be "cessation" there would have to be an "origin" and, as there is not, fear of dying dissolves in the equality of luminosity.

When investigated carefully there can be found no "things" at all and so appearing dissolves moment by moment in expanse.

This dissolving in no way impedes further appearing but remains always as the luminous ground, an equality of all seeming phenomena.

Because there are no "things" there is no meaning to a word such as "origin."

Because appearing is without origin it is free from taint, a stainless expanse like the sky.

This expanse is a triune dynamic experienced by the mature mind as a meaning-fullness, as bliss and as love (Dharmakaya, Sambhogakaya, Nirmanakaya).

To mature the mind beyond its superstitious belief in what might be called "things" and liberate it in-as this dynamic expanse is the purpose of all Dharma's many methods.

Kanchika

I removed a thorn from my heart
its name was

      Knowledge and Ignorance.

I saw the face of love.
now i do not care for philosophies

    but only
    the call of night birds,
    the darkness of shadows.

I came to you through the back garden. The night jasmine
languishing over brick wall had no argument with
the sureness of my touch and

the gardenias, (that favored sister of coffee)
with their whispered ballad of moonlight; well,

my intent was not lost on them.

The whole garden conspired that green night   and
sunlight obliged with its disappearance.

"the Lord awoke, like a strong man, powerful but
reeling with wine." 78th Psalm

The son of Mary on the cross, his face battered bloodied,
shone like a thousand suns as the spirit within him
soared like a falcon set lose from the kings arm.

Beauty is not carnal though it does inhabit, incarnate.
A guest in flesh and sinew; not like a trapped bird caged –
but like a friend whose presence enbrightens your home.

All of this world emerges from the beautiful, is not elsewhere than
the good – but the eye can be confused by the mind.
A man can think himself someone else – mental illness
does not take into account reality.

Last night's storm whipped through the woods, tore at
leaves, broke whole branches. My heart rejoiced.
I don't want to live in some protected place but inside
the lightning flash – the brilliance!

The Nazarene, Patrul, Yunus surrendered to that wind,
lived within lightning's burn. It's a pretty good bet that
a single tear from their cheek is the secret

of philosopher's stone.

On Study of Dharma: Alchemy

The unexamined life is not worth living.
                                    – Socrates, Apology 38a

All dharma teachings are *siddhi*. The very words, far beyond their linguistic meanings, are Gnostic utterances containing direct divulgence of wisdom.

> During a phase transition of a given medium certain properties of the medium change, often discontinuously, as a result of some external condition, such as temperature, pressure, and others. For example, a liquid may become gas upon heating to the boiling point, resulting in an abrupt change in volume. The measurement of the external conditions at which the transformation occurs is termed the *phase transition*.
>   – Wikipedia, "Phase Transition"

Dharma is conveyed in a series of propositions that describe "the view." In our tradition the process of dharma is cultivated in the order – view, meditation and action. To understand the alchemy of dharma propositions is a subtle and powerful wisdom. In the Zen tradition, there is an emphasis on transmission outside words and scriptures, a direct Gnostic transmission. Within the Tantric Buddhist tradition, scriptures themselves are used as carrying agents for trans-linguistic transmission outside words or scriptures. Tantra wishes to benefit beings of all levels of understanding. Many can only connect with words and scriptures while others can delve into the transmission beyond words and scriptures; Tantra serves both through the two levels of alchemical processing of teachings.

Dharma is comprised of a series of propositions. All systems are as is ordinary life, though in ordinary life most people's propositions are uninspected and gathered from the combinations of habit and external conditionings – these days mostly advertising. An advertising controlled consumerist society relies on this unconscious collecting of life propositions. Unexamined they form a mass of superstitions, often chaotic and contradictory, by which one lives – everything from "things can make you happy" to the superstitions birth and death.

Tantric Buddhism and all spiritual systems rely on a series of propositions, axioms, a coherent view within which the practices function. This is part of why it seldom works to mix systems. The methods work within the framework of the system and in reliance on the axioms. None of the methods are Truth. The propositions are also not Truth, they are the structure of a series of psychophysical maneuvers that alchemically transform the body and mind into a system that can directly, Gnosticly, know Truth. The Truth known has always been said to be beyond the reach of words and concepts.

How to work with such propositions so as to not only understand the linguistic word definitions but the spiritual power and transmission beyond words contained within them begins with the process of calcination. Calcination in industry, and in alchemy, is the process of thermal treatment, applying heat, to bring about phase transition. In alchemy calcination is first of a series of maneuvers in the production of the philosopher's stone. An understanding of the process of calcination in the study of dharma materials is vital to discover the alchemy of view. The unpacking of a dharma proposition has two fundamental phases: 1. consideration, 2. contemplation. I enjoy watching my dog, a small cavalier, run off with a bone and go to work on it. Every time

I see her chew and chew, single pointedly, until every bit is swallowed, I think of dharma study. The propositions of dharma should be chewed like this, eaten, digested. Buddha's teachings are living force which needs to be deeply considered. You are not asked for blind faith but to chew, hear the argument, consider it in relation to your life, consider its meaning and implications. No authentic teacher is worried about questions of any sort, they have no defensiveness with relation to the teachings. The teachings have shown their truth in the laboratory of their own human experience and that of many others.

Chew, consider, fight if you wish, argue, consider again. In the end, life and experience will eventually prove Buddha right ... or, you may discover this is simply not the path for you. Perhaps its axioms make no sense, in which case it is fine to go and search for a path which does. Longchenpa wrote, "Buddhas and Bodhisattvas manifest in accord with the needs of beings." There are many manifestations of varying forms, and not all paths are suited to all people. So consider at the level of intellect. In Tantra you are asked to work with body, speech (which includes the whole feeling dimension) and mind. One of the meanings of the word Tantra is to weave, to weave body, speech and mind into a single force of liberation. When you have considered deeply and feel you have a sense of what the proposition means in your life, as well as its corollary implications, then you can begin phase two. There is no end to the consideration of phase one; if you were to take any dharma proposition and consider it to its fullness you would end up with a total understanding of everything and the realization of the enlightened state.

In phase two you bind the proposition to mind and heart. This means you hold its meaning in silent single pointed concentration. The process of consideration prepares the linguistic formulation as an alchemical substance in your mind. Now you simply hold it, with great delicacy, in the silence of mind and heart. Much like a koan you hold it in great concentration; the Zen master Hakuin said you hold the koan as if you have swallowed a molten iron ball and it is burning through everything from the inside out. Knowing that the proposition holds an endless transmission of wisdom, and that the linguistic meaning is merely the price one pays for entering the inner dimension of it, you hold it in great pregnant expectancy. Like a mother about to give birth, you wait knowing you cannot force. Consideration lights the fire, and the pressure of this binding, holding in silence without looking for anything, begins the process of calcination. The package, the linguistic material begins to break down. The rasa, the vectoral disposition or flavor of feeling, of the linguistic meaning is released as volatile wafting essences to be absorbed and integrated. This integration allows the blessing to fill one. Here it is useful to understand that the word blessing in Tibetan does not merely have the sense of being patted on the head by a patriarch, but rather has the alchemical sense of a force which transforms one thing into another.

As one moves through the foundational axioms of the path, such as the four noble truths, four thoughts that turn the mind to dharma, four immeasurables, six perfections, they begin to function synergistically to transform the whole way body, mind, feeling know, feel. Perhaps an example would be useful of how this synergy works.

The Four Thoughts That Turn the Mind to Dharma

1. Precious Human Birth 2. Impermanence 3. Karma 4. The potential ceaselessness of suffering.

When understood fully, alchemically these four remove most of the structures that cause obstacles for successful practice of spiritual life. Often people simply rush through the preliminary consideration, but these contain great power, siddhi, and blessing of the Buddhas and sages of all times. Precious Human Birth is the first of these four and has dramatic meaning. Human birth is not in and of itself precious in this sense. Like all of Buddha's teachings, it offers great possibility, but is also an argument with human confusions The preciousness being referred to here is given as a potentiality that must be acted on to become actual. The mere fact of being born is not enough to insure the preciousness of human life. To exist is not to live in Truth but it does open the doorway. What makes a human birth precious? The possibility of moving beyond delusion, of attaining enlightenment for the sake of all sentient beings. Precious Human Birth is a gift and a demand. It is the demand that we not waste the opportunity. If it wasted then a great tragedy has happened. It is like a king who becomes lost and confused and wanders thinking he is a beggar.

A human being is a unique configuration of processes which allows realization of Buddhahood, enlightenment, more easily than any other configuration of being. Not gods, animals, hell realm beings, can match the uniqueness of the human configuration for swift and deep realization. An oak tree produces many, thousands upon thousands, of acorns over its life of a hundred years or so. Very few become oak trees; some are eaten by squirrels, some become compost for the soil, some sprout and die, others are eaten by birds or are collected by kids and end up in a dresser drawer somewhere. Many humans are born but very few seek the fullness of human birth's meaning. Those who have become dissatisfied with a partial life, those who long for something more can be said to have Precious Human Birth. If one contemplates Precious Human Birth to the point of cracking open its linguistic structure and contemplating its meanings, if one absorbs the essence of its meaning, then it will destroy even the possibility of meaninglessness. One may still suffer from frustration, dissatisfaction and the like, one may even suffer from brain chemistry related depression, but one will never doubt again that life has great meaning, great possibility.

He who has a why can endure any how. – Nietzsche

The second of the four thoughts is impermanence. All things are impermanent; they come to an end. All opportunities exist only for a limited time. Including Precious Human Birth. If you have contemplated the proposition called "Precious Human Birth" to the point of alchemical understanding then you will feel aghast at the thought of losing this chance. It is tremendously hard to keep the fact of death present in our minds. When we do, even at an ordinary level, it brings great poignancy and beauty to our field of experience. To consider the fact of our own personal impermanence to the point of alchemical integration with its meaning destroys the structure of complacency, procrastination and laziness within a human being.

The third of the four thoughts is karma. Karma is the vectoral momentum of habit, pure and simple. Newton's first law says: Every object in a state of uniform motion tends to remain in that state of motion unless an external force is applied to it. However it happened is beside the point, but now you are a motion of mixed wisdom and confusion. Today is arisen from yesterday's momentum. If you wish tomorrow to be different than today you must do something different. You must introduce an equal or greater force. Dharma and its unsullied wisdom is that force, but it must be applied. How is it applied? Through the methods of the path. The methods of the path are configurations of energy designed so as to be able to enter the human system as a force applied to transform habit. We must transform negative habit, which consumes our energy and attention robbing us of the chance for liberation. We transform negative habit into virtue habit, which releases energy and attention, so as to go beyond all habit into pristine stainless Original Innocence and Bright Virtue. The third of the four thoughts is where existentialism and Buddhism meet. Nature and nurture, essentialist and existentialist, genetics and environment are all co-emergent from the ground of awareness. The seeming dichotomy of these is purely illusory.

The alchemical consideration of the third thought that turns the mind to dharma removes the structures of self pity, resentment, blaming others and the tremendous waste of energy and time these entail. It places the responsibility for our lives squarely on our own shoulders. It does not say we have not been formed by events and circumstances often seemingly outside our control, but it says we can shape our minds, our response, our life and our actions – today. The great existentialist psychologist Viktor Frankl said:

> Everything can be taken from a man but one thing: the last of human freedoms – to choose one's attitude in any given set of circumstances, to choose one's own way.
> – *Man's Search for Meaning*

By declaring that man is responsible and must actualize the potential meaning of his life, I wish to stress that the true meaning of life is to be discovered in the world rather than within man or his own psyche, as though it were a closed system. I have termed this constitutive characteristic "the self-transcendence of human existence." It denotes the fact that being human always points, and is directed, to something or someone, other than oneself – be it a meaning to fulfill or another human being to encounter. The more one forgets himself – by giving himself to a cause to serve or another person to love – the more human he is and the more he actualizes himself. What is called self-actualization is not an attainable aim at all, for the simple reason that the more one would strive for it, the more he would miss it. In other words, self-actualization is possible only as a side-effect of self-transcendence.

– Man's Search for Meaning

The fourth of the four thoughts is the fact that suffering will not cease on its own. There is no savior coming to release us magically. There is no harmonic convergence, end of the Mayan calendar, dolphin ride, star ship from the Pleiades that will change us automatically. From this point forward physical evolution will continue unconsciously, but psychological evolution must proceed consciously. It is up to you and you alone.

Life is the flight of the alone to the alone.

– Plotinus, Enneads

Each proposition of dharma is a living force to be eaten, internalized, integrated as a change in disposition, character, action. Authentic changes in the level of knowledge require a co-emergent change in the level of one's being. To approach dharma study as an alchemical activity, and their blessing force as an alchemical agent, bears great fruit.

> The essence of all phenomena is the awakened mind;
> This very awakened mind is the mind of all the Buddhas;
> And the life spirit of every sentient being is this
> awakened mind as well.
> – *The Direct Experience of Kuntuzangpo's Mind Tantra*

> Until grasping of mind cease within the expanse of
> stainless space,
> The karmas of cause and result manifest as experience
> and
> Are added upon by the activities of mind.
> All these phenomena occur in mind, the mind creates,
> names, experiences,
> So in order to subdue self created sufferings of delusion,
> be diligent!
> – Longchenpa

An Aside on the Nature of Awareness

Often here it is said "essence and nature of your awareness," and that phrase sometimes presents a certain problem. The ocean, in its vastness and energy includes the wave, and the wave is not made of anything except ocean, but it can not quite be said that the wave includes the vastness and power of the whole ocean. The whole of me includes the hair on my arm, but the hair on my arm does not include the whole of me. I can pull one off throw it away and there is no loss. The individual "you" is made of nothing in reality … and that nothing is Original Innocence and Bright Virtue. The individual consciousness does *not* experience the wholeness of the essence and nature and can not. When the fixation on the individual aspect is dissolved, then awareness, in its ownmostness, experiences the body mind without separative identification or identity.

So they are the essence and nature of your awareness but not in the sense of them "being yours." The essence and nature can not be a subset, an object of ownership – or even experience, – of the separative identity. "You" cannot experience them or "know" them. You cannot "rest" in the presence of awareness. You can not find the presence of awareness. You are a subset of awareness, awareness is not a subset of "you" and your experience. If mind, in its separative identity based functions of conceptuality, rests in awareness then mind is gone. Then mind goes where no mind goes, and there there is no "personal mind," no "identity," no "self" location of perception and consciousness. As Milarepa once said "I do not see consciousness, awareness sees."

It is common to hear Dzogchen teachers talk of finding the presence of awareness these days. Or of "resting in the presence of awareness." But this is just silliness. Awareness has no presence. In fact it is characterized by an absence of presence. What dharma practice does is unstructured the rigidity of conceptual structures. When all concepts have been unraveled in this way what is left is a vast expanse of unutterable mystery, and within-as-of that, a pervasive luminous clarity. These give birth to the magical child of unceasing appearances. When the vast of awareness interfaces with a body mind without the meditation of consciousness, then it simply shines in-as-through that body mind without the self reflexive activity of a "me," "mine," "I," ... there is absolutely no "my awareness" sensation, concept or identity. So long as that is there, then one may be finding and resting in this or that expanded sensation or experience of self-reflexive consciousness but not in awareness. Such ease can be lovely but one must continue on and on journeying deeper on this flight of the alone to the alone

The Kiss of Sunlight

This morning the sunlight kisses the mist over the mountains and the mist dissolves saying, "Yes, yes!" The little creek flowing from the pond spills into the river, losing itself, and you can hear its sigh of love. The river will lose itself into a larger river and this into the ocean, only to be caught up by the sun's rays.

Once a small river was traveling across a great distance to the sea. On its journey it came to the edge of the desert and found it could not flow through the heat and sand. From above the sun spoke to it saying, "Dissolve into me and I will carry you out across the desert." The stream, of course, was frightened. To the stream this seemed like dying, it seemed like craziness and foolhardiness in the extreme. But something in the sun's whisper touched the river's heart. Something about the sun's beauty seduced it, called to its true essence, and it gave itself up into the sun's brilliance. Drawn into the sky the moisture traveled across the desert as cloud and, on the other side, fell as life-giving rain back down to the earth to become a stream again.

We are like this. We are the stream flowing toward the ocean of enlightenment and we are stopped at the edge of samsara's desert. The All Good Mother, Buddha, whispers in our ear, "I have a way. Come, listen to my words, walk my path." Can we let our hardened hearts melt in the warm rays of compassion? Can we let our form, our insistence of concretizing everything, slip away and take on the sublime intangible forms of wisdom brilliance?

an unbrokenness not a totality made up of parts or
even a wholeness discrete single but
a mystery beyond numbers or words.

the mystery of lived experience irreducible
to location devoid of
                localization
                subjectivity
                externality.
the tender heartedness of a meaningful expanse.

i come to you, you to me, in the unexplainability
of love
        an always opening out
        the accumulation of immediacies
and we grow old together in this unbrokeness
of me you us – not me not you not us
mystery irreducible
love.

Our love is found in the bone, flesh, muscle. Our love is in the plants we grow to eat, the deep woods where we wander, the engine sound of the tractor. Our love is in the movement of mystery where eye meets smile, where guest meets host, where other becomes beloved. In the end we live our life fearlessly into everything and every "thing" until there are no more things – only love. To me that is the meaning of spiritual life – this incarnation of beauty, truth, goodness and love. Realize this most subtle understanding and live it into all appearing.

q. – Often you refer to this mystery and its luminous nature as "divine" – why is that?
t. – Within the continuum of the highest all terms such as "highest" and "divine" are irrelevant. There is only Silence, a luminous divine Silence. But, in terms of the karmic body, the feelings, the mind's functions – when realization, and abidance in-as-of the highest, is realized it is felt as what we mean by the words "divine," "absolute," "sublime," "freedom," "love."

Desire, Longing and Spiritual Maturity

1. There is suffering. 2. There is a cause of suffering.
3. There is an end to suffering. 4. There is a path to
that end.

Once you have imbibed the existential force of the first and
second noble truths, and only then, the third and fourth
noble truths arise as a great and tremendous happy longing
into enlightenment.

In between pure delusion and great awakening is the
path of spiritual maturing. Ultimately, all desire must be
transformed, but not all desire is the same or equally problematic. There is worldly desire that leads to more confusions, and spiritual desire that leads to wisdom. The desires
that lead to wisdom should be carefully cultivated and the
desires that lead to confusions should be purified. One
moves from confused desire to wisdom desire in order to go
beyond all desire. Without this progressive movement resulting from a careful consideration of the teachings, all talk
of going beyond desire is fantasy. And spiritual fantasy is the
shallowest sort of delusion.

Worldly desire gives form, structure, and shape to mind
and causes mind to lose its natural connection with purity,
lose its inherence in and as the mystery of reality. Because
the mind and heart are confused as to the authentic essence
and nature of awareness, it becomes involved in desires born
from ignorance and it endlessly spins the wheel of samsara
through multiple lifetimes. But always the intrinsic wisdom
is there; never separate, although it is obscured by confusion and ignorance and darkened by delusion. Suffering is a
very patient teacher. It is in moments when we are suffering
that we have the greatest possibility of intuiting our greater

potential. When we are weary with the endless alternations of good and bad moments in life, tired of pop music love songs and the shopping channel, and we find ourselves wondering about how to live a life of greater meaning and depth, we begin to mature in such a way as to be able to make use of a path. Those desires born from thinking about life's deep meaning and the deep longing for truth can't be realized through passing, impermanent things and relations, which lead only to more grasping confusion and disappointment. When one begins to recognize all desires as symbols of the longing for truth, and directs their energy toward this longing, then desire becomes fuel for the path. Then one can learn to turn any activity into wisdom and bliss. We must close the door to idiocy and allow the energy that was previously wasted pursuing confused desires to accumulate until it reaches a point where it opens another door. Within this waiting state one can engage the methods of the path that will forge body, feeling and mind into an alchemical cauldron to hold transformative energies. Otherwise, energy poured into this cauldron flows back out like water poured into a sieve.

It takes great maturity before the random desiring of the confused mind begins to awaken beyond the illusion of concepts' false structures. When someone matures enough to realize that happiness seemingly created by any object, relationship or circumstance is inherently problematic, that "made happiness" is always eventually unmade, then one begins to awaken beyond the lure of egoic desiring and its endlessly marketed illusion of satisfaction. When this happens, when the dynamic force of the divine, inherent already in everything, begins to function due to human maturity, a tremendous longing for spiritual understanding arises from the sorrow of seeing the human realm in all its shallowness. The heart longs for something more, something greater. This longing is desire beginning to be drawn into wisdom.

It is like a magnifying glass that a child uses to focus the sun's rays and set fire to dry grass. Spiritual longing focuses desire's randomness and allows it to set fire to delusion.

Methods of an authentic path and the blessings of authentic guru are the focusing of mind's wisdom sun. These two, once they are discovered, create a wish to grow within the structure of one's life, and this wish to grow, this longing for truth, has great power. I recall the Sufi saint Kabir who said, "On this path of truth, longing does almost all the work," and that is so very true. It is by harnessing the energy of random fears, hopes and desires and bringing them into the wish to grow that one gives birth to what might be referred to as a "Chief Steward" within psyche. The Chief Steward is an aspect of one's psyche that has the ability to draw all the randomness of body, mind, feelings and whims into a coherent whole. It is the guardian of the wish to grow. If the Chief Steward is fed the energy from random confused desiring, it will become like the sun within the solar system holding the planets, random mental and emotional habits, in a chosen orbit. The secret of this possibility is the ability to turn all desire into spiritual longing – to redefine what it is we are truly longing for.

Those who are emotionally anemic, emotionally immature or excessively wounded at the level of feeling, have a very hard time with spiritual longing. Many pseudo non-dualists discount longing since everything is already Buddha. They cultivate a conceptual conceit of enlightenment that leads to radical indifference and has all the sparkling qualities of a dried out cornhusk. This is not enlightenment. Enlightenment is not indifferent to suffering beings. Authentic realization is always the paradoxical union of the utterly transcendent essence, the luminous nature of bliss and the ceaseless appearing as love; these are the essence, nature and energy of awareness. As my Guru used to say, Nirmanakaya (the appearing aspect of awareness) is love, and love is deeply involved, caring, attentive – the activity of compassion. Love loves to love. That is simply what it does. It is its nature, activity and quality. If one has wisdom awareness of the non-dual then one's body lives to love. Love also embraces longing; the longing of Buddhas is to express this love.

The depth and intensity of spiritual longing and desire is directly proportional to the maturity of each person and their outgrowing of deluded, ignorant desire. This is important to understand. Not all desiring is the same. Not all seeking is the same. These days spiritually ignorant pseudo non-dualists speak of "no seeking," but the only seeking and desiring they are truly counseling anyone to give up is spiritual seeking. If you give up spiritual longing before it has burned away all ordinary concepts and desires then all you do is fall into a stupor of abstracted indifference based in rejecting wisdoms qualities. Until even the last concept is purified in expanse there should be longing, and longing seeks union with the object of its attention. After that no one needs to tell you seeking is wrong because you have realized – made real in body, mind, feeling – the truth. So, people with all kinds of desire, chockfull of desire, come to so-called spiritual teachers who tell them to give up seeking, to stay in the "now" and give up all efforts to seek. But then these people give up spiritual longing and seeking and go seeking all manner of ordinary mundane things according to the whims of mind, mind's deluded concepts. The only thing they give up is spiritual seeking and spiritual longing! They cut the life vein of the earliest stirring of their spiritual awakening and spill the blood of it onto the ground of ordinary desire.

If you have given up all desires, then yes, spiritual longing and desire will dissipate as well. It won't have to be forced, it happens naturally. In the same way as when you put fire into a hollow log and the fire burns up the log and then is extinguished. Spiritual longing awakens as the first dawn rays of the fully enlightened state, and then the methods, along with the blessing of guru and lineage, focus those rays until they become a blazing wisdom fire. Medicine is not needed in the natural state of health but it restores one to it, and when the illness is gone the medicine is gone as well. Here the illness is confusion about desire, ego, separation, the relationship between appearance and emptiness, between the divine and all appearances. The path is what clarifies this confusion, and what it uses to fuel that process of clarifying is your longing and desire.

In non-dual traditions where there is no authentic realization, the conceptual conceit of enlightenment there is always a lot of talk talk talk talk. Satsang has become an occasion to spin words, concepts and ideas about non-duality into a haze of intellectual abstraction in which everyone pretends to understand what is being said and concludes that being able to parrot the words is enlightenment. But if we examine the qualities of such people, we can easily conclude that this is not enlightenment. Wisdom realization, shining like a thousand suns, that burns from head to toe is the fully enlightened state; it is beyond ordinary and spiritual longing, but it awakens in body-mind-feeling another longing, the longing of compassion to liberate beings lost in suffering. At this stage of realization all longing becomes love, the radiance of awareness as energy. Love of appearing, of beings, of appearance as expression of the divine wisdom bliss. This love longs for all beings to know its own state. It longs into action, the actions of compassion, longs into appearance, incarnates and moves in wind, word, flesh, action.

Enlightenment is everywhere, in your hands, your feet, in the marrow of your bones, in all of the world and its appearance inseparable from the mysterious purity of the divine essence. Until the world itself is translated into wisdom bliss only, there is not full realization and longing goes on as the inherent intelligence of that dynamic wisdom. After this translation, longing becomes sunlight, the poetry of spring rain, the expanse of blue sky.

This longing you feel is your most precious possession. Yes, you should not let it be co-opted by ordinary desire, and you should not make it into an accumulation of bliss, visions, spiritual experiences and other such useless stuff. That is not the meaning or function of the authentic spiritual path where the distinction between experience and wisdom is always discovered. Mostly, the ones who tell you to give up spiritual seeking simply return you to the deluded market-place world of their ego driven chatter, Facebook ejaculated opinions and spiritual internet website shopping cart apps. Do not be seduced by this falsity. Burn with longing, give shape and fuel to that longing through the methods of the path. When path, ego and longing desire all disappear in the wisdom dawn of the fully enlightened state there is no more question of giving up this or that. The very question is outshone in the brilliance of wisdom bliss.

The Baul mystics of Bengal say submission is the secret of knowledge. Submission of the ego's logic of separation and territories into the wisdom longing and method of authentic spirituality. Then you will not know the unborn wisdom, be-cause to know it there would have to be separation, but you dissolve into that mystery and become mystery only. You look at your hand and it is pure mystery of emptiness and divinity. You look at your foot and it has become Buddha. Then you will know again all appearances without confusion and they will be seen, lived and loved as the nonbinding play of beauty and wonder, and you will be able to act as com-passion in the midst of confusion. This is the real import of your longing. Your most precious procession, this longing desire, is a wish fulfilling jewel beyond all price. Don't trade it for the shallow consolation of spiritual concepts.

before there was any shrouding

there is a view
long,
expanse.

the mood of lucency before the notion color.
a scenario of love before the notion other.
and that is how I met you
without the boundary of "one" or "two."

this was the primordial state of affairs

Haha! Still Here

Each morning the body of the sage wakes and thinks Haha!
Still here.

3 AM mind wanders across the field of emptiness and
affection.
 In the deep sleep state the sage rests in their natural
expanse as Dharmakaya. Scientists have a hard time under-
standing why we need deep sleep. A sage knows it is because
the iceberg tip of mind as concept dissolves into the vast
expanse of wholeness in deep sleep. Mind resolves, dissolves,
rests, frolics in ease as nothingness. Body absorbs the joy of
mind's rest without cares in itsownmost expanse of birthless
and deathless ease.

4 AM mind stops to rest at the threshold of nighttime and
dawn, that liminal moment when empty luminosity becomes
the variegated appearance called life.
 Right at the moment of waking the yogi who practices
the nighttime yoga of luminosity becomes able to witness the
arising of forms without ever leaving the expanse. Ramana
Maharshi once said the jnani *(sage) is like someone in deep*
sleep all the time. Awareness never leaves the expanse to
become partial consciousness as identity and identification.
As Milarepa said, "I don't see consciousness I see aware-
ness."Awareness as expanse simply perceives everything, like
planets floating in its own expanse, and the planets are just
made up of awareness' ornaments.

5 AM mind rests in union and 6 AM mind is training with breath.
 As the body awakens from deep sleep, the luminous thread
of awareness is not lost and all appearance, body, the world,

subtle and gross appearances are seen as the single body of life.
They are the single manifestation, play, of awareness' poten-
cy and creativity. As body awakens more fully, breath pulls
prana *into body. Air fills lungs and prana moves through the*
body's channels. Mind trains in silence and stillness, riding the
breath, simply being with-in-as-body in-as-of awareness' ex-
panse. The incarnation of awareness takes place, and compas-
sion finds a home here, everywhere.

This whole human realm appearance is a complicated
tendency, and if it were not for the tender hearted affection
that reaches, stretches, twists and turns itself into its self and
other (mind you, without ever leaving the empty ground of
Nothingness), there would be little to recommend it. But it
does, and here we are! Me to you, you to me, neither being
nor non being, empty yet appearing … and no rigged (or
rigid) philosophy, no conceptual contrivance, can circum-
scribe a circle to hold this beauty in.

7 AM mind meets waitress approaching table with eggs and
toast. (It seems Love has no boundary when the smile is
genuine.)
    Buddha once said, "In thirty years I have never taken
a step or said a word." Abiding as the Nothingness state, the
body moves, talks, acts from the radiance of awareness; playful
energy of compassion, wisdom, bliss without any intention at
all. It acts without any actor. When this happens then body
is animated by love. As body moves through appearing, with
ease, it feels nothing but a vast and tender-hearted love for all
appearances. It only sees Buddhas in a Buddha realm of beauty.

8 AM mind feels gearshift and pedal, traffic pattern and flow.
Sense and sense field meet in the love play of Bodhisattvas
and outside the car window …

In Tantra one comes to understand, through the practices of vajra body, *that all appearance is the play of Buddhas in union. Sense and sense field are Bodhisattvas in union. Eye meets form and there is only the love play of intimate lovers. Sound to ear, hand to touch. Everywhere as far as the eye can see, perception is pure pleasure. The aggregates of the body, form, feeling, perception, consciousness and formation, are known as male Buddhas, and the elements of the body as female Buddhas; and these aggregates and elements are engaged in the most delightful frolic of pleasure and joy. Everything is union. Everything is bliss and wisdom divulging itself, emptiness and clarity giving birth to joy in form.*

9AM mind is the union of dynamic immensity and golden fields of wheat. (Oh that love could be formed to word! That hand could paint this mystery or feet dance its simple imponderable wonder ... all these will be tried and tried again because wave is communication, song bird, eye's glance, feel of road rushing under ...... mystery demands contact and communication and so) ...
When mind rests in the absolute, the Nothingness State, body is simply animated by love. Love has a deep desire to communicate itself. The body longs into communication of its unborn and undying wisdom and bliss. The body appears in the word for the joyous task of speaking, dancing, painting, farming, making, doing, becoming into expression of wisdom bliss. It can never perfectly describe enlightenment – no words or acts can – but it does enjoy the trying.

10 AM mind sitting by the side of a road writing this, sunlight on the creek, mind slipped beyond itself into the empty wonder and infinity again sings into emptiness while vastness lives to virtue through cell, bone, muscle, sinew, life breath and word.

Later, evening will come on its sure and silent feet, mind will sink and fall into expanse. No consciousness, no unconsciousness, just mystery.

All day the sage, as body and appearance, abides as the act of expression, expressing wisdom bliss, and at night they lay down the body and its cares and fall into the vast of perfect mystery untouched even by expression. Each morning the body of the sage wakes and thinks Haha! Still here.

Freedom and Obligation

student: Rinpoche, with respect, your freedom, to me, looks like tons and tons of obligation – speaking as a person who is very lazy! How does it feel like freedom to you? Why would you use that word? I thought I would ask this because I constantly struggle with choices between "freedom" and "obligation" and I have never met someone who takes on as many obligations as you. I know in my heart that laziness is not freedom but I still struggle in an ongoing way with this!

T: Do you know this old Zen story? A young novice comes to the master and asks, "How do we deal with the endless demands of waking, sleeping, eating, shitting … ?" And the master replies, "We wake, sleep, eat, shit, pee."

For me, even if the universe disappears this moment, I am not changed or affected in any way. Free from birth and death, free from mind, free from desire, free from body – I am free to live birth, death, to live the body as Love. Not free in body but to *live body, world, actions.* I am not *in* these, they are within that expanse called Nothingness that is the only identity. It is only in this way that one can be free to live Love's demands. The ocean does not need to be free from the wave; the wave is simply the natural rising falling of ocean. You do not ask how to be free from the lungs action, the beating of the heart, the work of the spleen. Why? Because you have not alienated yourself from these functions. You have separated, in mind and habit only, yourself from life, world and others, your so-called obligations, and so you have turned them into a hardship. I have no alienation so I do not share this burden.

What freedom is there in your laziness? What freedom is there in being pulled willy-nilly by the demands of the lazy mind, forever unable to accomplish the noble goals you once envisioned – remember the Bodhisattva vow? What freedom is there in struggle? What freedom is there in being a slave to the body, to middle class values with all their hidden ugliness and social/personal discontent, to consumerism's marketing plan? I look at your freedom and I only see slavery. Not a slave of Love, a slave to middle class human conditioning. I look and I remember the great saint Kabir's words, "The Lord of Love asks for a head. I look at your life and I wonder why you are not jumping up to offer yours?"

What freedom is there when unborn wisdom awareness, unstained by suffering, without boundary of form, attribute, substance ...... mistakes itself for the tiny speck called body. Awareness, free and unborn, lives every appearance as a play, a joy, a frolic without ever being trapped or conditioned. See this hair on my arm? It is me, but if I pull it out I am not harmed. The relationship of me with this body, and me with the whole of appearance is the same – a bit of a bit of straw blown off the roof into Nothingness. I take my stand as-in-of that Nothingness, and in the total freedom, and ease, the body simply lives love in whatever manner love chooses. It works just as the spleen works, the liver, the blood. If it chooses to do nothing and sit in a cave, or a theatre, then fine. If it chooses all the works it now does, fine. Its choice will not even come as choice but as perfect responsiveness to what ever arises.

You think choice is freedom but choice is just confusion. Informed, as it is, by wisdom and freedom, love and compassion, this body meets each situation and responds spontaneously from wisdom. The correct response is clear and to do anything else would require confusion. So really, this body lives in a choiceless state. And that is because mind rests in perfect freedom. You are so burdened by Being, and then the obligations of "having a body," that you tie yourself up in mental knots trying to avoid obligation in accord with your attraction, aversion and indifference. That is not freedom. There is no freedom *for* the body – there is freedom as the context of the content of all appearances. And then there is action *by* the body in accord with wisdom and love. I do not have a body – body is my expression of love, a dance step in wisdom's grand ballet of appearing.

The body only wishes to live as Love. It is the true longing, the true joy of body. Mind wishes to live in the freedom of non-being. It is the Only satisfaction. Feeling wishes to live as tender-heartedness without any touch of fear. When body is wisdom's expression these ideas you have will all drop away. Think it over. Buddha's argument is a fierce one that does not glorify American middle class slavery marketed as weekend, happy hour, vacation, retirement "Freedom."

The Techniques Do Not Work

The techniques do not work. Pure and simple. You work. The skillful means do not work. You work! Methods and techniques are dead verbiage and exotic calisthenics if they are divorced from context. It is the context of the womb that keeps the fetus alive. It is the context of your motivation and intention that keep the living force of spiritual transmission alive.

Do not be a street dog of dharma who grabs its bone and runs off snarling and biting at every passerby. Buddha Padmasambhava laid out the path in clear fashion. He explained the steps to follow in order to create an environment, a womb – a context, for healthy development of the fetus of realization. The path as a whole, the entire Buddhist way, from Sutra's renunciation to Tantra's third conduct and Dzogchen's "no remedy," forms a single living organic whole. Each higher aspect rests upon the developmental foundation of the earlier stages the way a fetus grows from a few cells through many stages of evolutionary development into a human child.

Take for instance renunciation. Renunciation is the method of Sutra and there are lists of things to be given up, actions not to be engaged, feelings to be rejected. In Tantra's path of transformation these lists do not apply but this does not mean that renunciation has somehow been lost. In Tantra, renunciation becomes more subtle, more refined, and manifests as the renunciation of impure view and not the renunciation of this or that illusory object arisen from impure view. In Dzogchen's great openness one renounces straying from . Without authentic weariness for samsara's deceptive seduction the Tantrica's so-called view is only a cover for grasping and aggression, and the Dzogchenpa's relaxed attitude is simply a fretful sham. The view, vows, re-alization and accomplishments of each vehicle are contained within successively higher stages of sublime presentation. Weariness for samsara and profound compassionate love for all beings are the context for Mahayana's excellent path of virtue. These plus authentic faith in sublime wisdom beings are necessary for Tantra's skillful means to flower. Without these, Tantra's bevy of techniques will be nothing more than the pond into which Narcissus gazes, admiring himself in ever increasing alienation and isolation. Take the time to truly develop each quality of the path, such as authentic renunciation, compassion, faith and devotion so that from the context, the womb, of your life an authentic child of the noble family of dharma can be born.

The Beloved Came to My Bed

The beloved came to my bed and whispered in my ear, offered me a cup. Without question I gulped it down. Night fell but I was drunk on sunlight. The religion game is for those who care about gain and loss – but listen up preacher, I have already lost everything and if I found anything left I would give it away. Living inside the tousled hair of my beloved I peak out now and then at the coming and going of Being.

∾

The body has a great need for the immeasurable, a thirst. When the mind becomes still, silent – free from chaos – then the body is suddenly infused with an "otherness" whose sacred delicacy is unutterable joy. The body is held within its tenderness and that tenderness impacts perception with blessing. Perceiving becomes the act of abiding within, dwelling within holiness.

In the language of Dzogchen, mind's silent stillness is the essence. The otherness is the nature. The body is known as the energy which is love.

∾

There is no separation in the moonlight's love affair with the pine.

The impossibility of numbering

when mind has gone to silence, love pervades. appearing,
without implication of appearance. becomes the expanse
where namelessness dwells
in myriad guises, names, forms   and
even though perceiving implies   and
structure provokes,
in truth, not even the shadow of things ...... exists.

the gentle evenness of silence informs.
my hand, your hand ... warmth on warmth where
does one begin the other ......

if i say "two" i lie. if i say "one" the unease of not quite true.

The Unknown Bird:

...... return again) this knowledge of things acquired. the
divine also dwells – in becoming, in because. and in why.
in the poetic edda of this existence. dwells within
unknowing of things.
unmaking
of suredness.
the joy at the end of the day.

emptiness is intimacy. when known not as adjective but
verb. not intransitive but applying, always ...... everywhere,
to every "thing". unbecoming acquiring unmaking thingness.

re-turning again, the unknown bird flies
from somethingness to nothingness, from
noThingness to brightness   and

alights on the shoulder of the unofficial self.

He would come to live in your heart.
If your life were a one stringed instrument
if your knowing were an unmaking –
in the embrace of substanceless things.

(you could make him, that unknown bird ...

The Wisdom of Seeking

The Sufis have a slogan, "You can not attain enlightenment by seeking but no one except seekers ever attain enlightenment." This is so very true.

There are those in the current shallow pools of spiritual faddism who use the poetic utterance of the absolute to deny the need for any path or any seeking. Generally spiritually anemic, they proffer a castrated way whose verbiage covers over a deep ambivalence about the demands of hard work which the path requires. "Everything is perfect! Everything is Buddha already." They say, "If you seek you miss, for the Truth is right here and now." Of course the paradox, of all things always already being within the Buddha Nature *and* the need for a path to realize this, has been addressed since time immemorial. By and large those spiritual dilettantes of the "no seeking" school give up spiritual seeking, but their lives are nothing but the display of ordinary gross level seeking shaped by attraction, aversion and indifference.

The Vajrayana path, or Tantric Buddhism, begins with the fact that things are always already quite perfect. The true spiritual seeking that evolves from alchemical integration of longing is not a seeking for what is somewhere else, but merely the seeking to remove the blindfold that obscures direct seeing of reality – As It Is. Because of this Tantric Buddhism is called "the resultant path." This means that the result is there right from the start. The ground of the path and the end of the path are exactly the same with one big difference. The ground is Buddha Nature, the union of essence and nature, emptiness and clarity. The result is Buddha Nature, the union of essence and nature. The difference is that what obscured the body mind from knowing this, and living this knowing, has been removed.

Just because Buddha Nature is what everything is, sadly does not mean that everyone realizes this or lives in accord with this knowledge. If a person is standing at the edge of the Grand Canyon alongside of you, and you are saying how beautiful it is and they are saying, "I just don't see it?" you wonder "What is wrong?" You look over and see they are wearing a blindfold that obscures their vision of the beauty. So you suggest, "Hey, maybe take off that blindfold." They do and see the beauty. So the beauty was always already there but they were unable to see it due to temporary obstruction to clear seeing. Or, a man is named Eddie but he has a mental breakdown and thinks he is Napoleon. His obscurations are more subtle than the first man's blindfold and obscure reality both inner and outer. Now, you can walk up to him and say, "Hey bub, you're not Napoleon you are Eddie." This is very unlikely to help. It is a lack of ability to see his state clearly, and empathize, that makes someone think this would be a solution. In the same way you can say, "Hey bub, it's all Original Innocence and Bright Virtue. That's all there is!" but this fails to see what is obscuring others from seeing their true nature – the way that the veils to clear seeing are embodied and enworlded in the structures of the man's living.

At best, and this is the common result of that effort, you will encourage those who are a bit weak-minded to imitate the sages words and become lost in a double delusion – now also a delusion of being non-deluded.

My father's friend, who had a mental breakdown in WWII – of course he was always already Eddie, but if he didn't overcome his delusion and abide in the realization, making real his Eddieness in body, speech and mind, this fact of his always already Eddieness did him little good. If somehow, perhaps, these purveyors of shallowness actually knew there was no seeking needed, if they could dwell as body, mind, feeling in that state, then we would have to say they were sorely lacking in empathetic ability to see others clearly in terms of what they needed. Not everyone who attains realization of the natural state is also a teacher, guru, spiritual master ….. in fact most are not. That requires realization and skillful means to work with others. In that case they would do better to have an honest profession like baking bread or farming, and if they wished to teach take the time to learn how. Those who are born to the function, not status, of sharing the highest truth are naturally overflowing with skillful means. They are not lacking in empathy or skill, as these flow spontaneously from the expanse as the qualities of enlightenment. In Tibetan the word for Buddha is *Sangye*. It is made of two parts. The first means removal of all that obscures clear seeing of reality and the second means expansion of all good qualities.

Spiritual seeking comes with maturity that outshines ordinary grasping at confused dualistic objects. Spiritual paths of quality tend to make clear that the result is present from the start and that "seeking" experiences, states, whatever, is *not* the point of the path. The distinction between experience and wisdom is the very basis of our Nyingma path of meditation. So what is the spiritual path doing? It is taking off the blindfold so you can see all As It Is. This if course is a bit more difficult than taking off a blindfold because the blindfold is made up of the cloth of yourself. Your habits, concepts, patterns with which mind identifies itself, as itself, all make up the blindfold. Mind Itself, in its ownmostness, is made up of the union of emptiness and clarity and has no particular identity. It is not even confined within the identity of Being or Non-being; it is perfect unspeakable mystery known in the absence of any concepts. What is known is the Original Innocence and Bright Virtue, not as good idea or view but as direct Gnostic seeing or living vision. Taking off the blindfold of outer, inner and subtle identifications and allowing awareness to know itself in its ownmostness is the point of the path and of our Precious Human Birth.

This is important to understand because if one does not understand there is a need for the path, even though everything is always already Buddha Nature, then one will waste one's life. It is a not uncommon course of events that people will waste their lives, selectively reading Dzogchen or Advaita, using the absolute teachings to negate the need for efforts. One sees this often in the dilettante quality of internet spiritual discussions on Facebook where people quote Ramana Maharshi, Nisargadatta Maharaj and Dzogchen Tantras stating the need to give up all efforts, all seeking, all paths. They offer up these quotes from one part of the master's teaching and ignore the quotes on the need for efforts, the need for sincerely earnestly following the path. The result of all this sloppy, ego centered selective, ideational consideration of the path is jaded cynicism.

On the other hand, if one does not recognize the always already state of Buddha Nature as the origin and starting place of the path, then the path will tend to devolve into ordinary samsaric seeking for experiences and states. There is no doubt that there are better and worse relative states of experiences. There is nothing wrong with seeking out and enjoying basic states of pleasure and the like, but these will always be temporary at best and not satisfy the spiritual urge within us. That which is built up will fall apart, that which is gained anew can again be lost. The only thing which can offer happiness without the seeds of falling back into misery is a discovery of something that was always already the case but missed.

In Vajrayana, Tantric Buddhism, we say that appearances are not the problem but rather the viewing them other than how they actually are. Perceiving in a distorted fashion is the problem. This distortion of perception is embodied in our habits and enworlded in our social structure. Our work to purify our personal distortions of vision must take place, therefore, within the overall structure of our embodiment. Just talking will not do. Just pretending you are not Napoleon, when you feel absolutely convinced you are, will not do. You need to uncover what structures of thinking and feeling and embodiment cause this delusion. You must purify the habits of confused conceptuality and the manner in which these embodied and enworlded in your life. You must purify all concept; so long as a single concept remains there is bondage. This is the work of the path and, when it is accomplished, then you perceive things exactly as they are. In that moment, then always, waking or sleeping, you will abide as unborn and undying wisdom awareness and bliss – exactly what you have always been, Original Innocence and Bright Virtue.

My lips move,

sounds fly out. a secret script describing ......

Mind lost in love's unknowing can't predict what words will
come out. One day it is foolishness, another all gems.
Reason wants an audience, argumentation

knows gain and loss, but love's syllables fall like
droplets of shattered light across the geography called life.

Reason becomes mute when it first hears its first song
of love and unknowing. If it could find words they

would say things like:

"Inside this shirt, the moon and stars."

EPILOGUE

My hut lies in the middle of a dense forest;
every year the green ivy grows longer.
No news of the affairs of men,
only the occasional song of the woodcutter.
The sun shines and I mend my robe;
When the moon comes out I read Buddhist poems.
I have nothing to report to my friends.
If you want to find the meaning, stop chasing after
       so many things.

                 –Ryokan, *One Robe One Bowl*, 43

Permissions

The publisher and the author acknowledge that in cases where excerpts of Rumi poems in this book are uncredited, these pieces are taken from the author's personal notes, recorded over many years, in his conversations with his teachers along the way. While an attempt was made to locate the original sources, these were not found. Anyone knowing of the original source for these quotes is invited to contact the publisher so that credit may be assigned in future printings. Thank you.

Poem on pages 98-99:
"when serpents bargain for the right to squirm". Copyright 1948, (c) 1976, 1991 by the Trustees for the E E Cummings Trust. Copyright (c) 1979 by George James Firmage from COMPLETE POEMS: 1904-1962 by E.E. Cummings, edited by George J Firmage. Used by permission of Liveright Publishing Corporation.

Poems on pages 66, 132:
Ikkyû, ["you poor sad thing thinking death is real"] and ["born born everything is always born"] from *Crow With No Mouth*, versions by Stephen Berg. Copyright © 1989, 2000 by Stephen Berg. Reprinted with the permission of The Permissions Company, Inc., on behalf of Copper Canyon Press, www.coppercanyonpress.org.

Poem on pages 135-136:
"Acts of Helplessness" by Jelal al-din Rumi, from *The Essential Rumi*, translated by Coleman Barks with John Moyne, New York: Harper Collins edition, 1996. Used with permission.

CONTACT INFORMATION

TRAKTUNG YESHE DORJE is an American born spiritual teacher who has taught in the U.S., Cuba, and Europe since 1990. For twenty-two years he has guided the Tsogyelgar spiritual community outside Ann Arbor, Michigan. His root guru—Lama Thinley Norbu Rinpoche—encouraged him to write so as to clarify Vajrayana Buddhism for Western audiences. He has guided the creation of America's largest mural of Tantric art, and overseen the creation of a Western form of *doha* songs (celebrations of spiritual teaching), now on several CDs. He is president of Wishing Tree Gardens, a non-profit sustainable-agriculture educational program.

Contact Information: www.traktung.org

HOHM PRESS is committed to publishing books that provide readers with alternatives to the materialistic values of the current culture, and promote self-awareness, the recognition of interdependence, and compassion. Our subject areas include parenting, transpersonal psychology, religious studies, women's studies, the arts and poetry.

Contact Information: Hohm Press, PO Box 4410, Chino Valley, Arizona, 86323; USA; 800-381-2700, or 928-636-3331; email: hppublisher@cableone.net www.hohmpress.com